When Perfection
Isn't Perfect

Michael G Farrell

May God's Purpose in your life shine bright for the world to see. Remember to find One Good Thing each day... If you can't find one... Be the good for someone.

Barefoot Kicker #15

CONTENTS

Introduction

Mike was originally recruited by Tom Heckert, then the head football coach at Adrian College. I took over for Coach Heckert in April of 1982 and continued recruiting all the guys Coach had on his list, including a young kicker from Fenton, Michigan, Mike Farrell. When you recruit punters and kickers it is more about their stats than anything else. I looked at Mike's high school stats, and they were good, not great. We had a kicker for one more year and after speaking with Mike I thought he may be able to improve enough to be our kicker. So, I wanted him at Adrian. When Mike came into camp, it was the first time I had met him, he seemed very quiet, that was not unusual for a freshman. It was a rather intimidating situation for a young guy. I remember Mike coming and asking for a bag of balls to use on Sunday during our day off during camp. I was not sure what his deal was, but I loved guys that wanted to do extra work. Little did I know that he was having trouble with his kicking and that was the weekend he decided to go barefoot. Mike did not kick at all his freshman year and looked like he would be our kicker going into 1983. Somehow, we ended up with a kicker from Northern California by the name of Frank Runyon. Mike and he battled during camp, we put them in all sorts of competitions. We decided that Mike would be our kicker. Ended up a good choice. In 1983, Mike's first game he kicked 3 field goals and we would win 9-7. We had our secret weapon. Mike would go on that year to be 17 for 17 in extra points and 12 for 21 in field goals, be the All

MIAA Kicker, and be a part of an MIAA Championship team, along with being in the National Playoffs. In 1984 Mike would be 30 for 30 in extra points and 5 for 8 in field goals and again be All MIAA as the kicker. In 1985, he would be more of the same, he would be 37 for 37 in extra points and again 5 for 8 in field goals and for the third year in a row he would be All MIAA kicker. It should be mentioned that Mike had the same snapper for three years, Steve Bohl and he had two holders, Jeff Hood for 1983 and Steve Konkle for 1984 and 1985. Mike and Steve had been working on a fake extra point. Where Steve would take the ball on the snap and go down the line of scrimmage, if no one there he would go into the endzone, if he got pressure, he would pitch to Mike. I told them we would not run it unless we were up four touchdowns. In our last game in 1985, we would get up four touchdowns and even before we scored, Mike was by my side, Coach can we do it, almost begging. I said yes, Konkle takes the ball down the line of scrimmage and could have gone into the endzone but instead he pitches to our barefoot kicker, Mike catches the ball and has to dive over two guys trying to tackle him into the endzone for a two-point conversion. I had never seen Mike happier. Over the years there have not been many players from Adrian or from any MIAA school that have been All MIAA for three years in a row. Mike would finish his career 84 for 84 in extra points, the only division 3 player to finish with an 100% over 50 kicks, he would finish 22 for 37 in field goals for 60% and made several important field goals over the years. In 2009 Mike would be inducted into the Adrian College Hall of Fame, a big honor for the quiet kicker from Fenton, Michigan. As Mike became our go-to guy for field goals and extra points, he grew as a person. He became much more confident, much more involved with the other players, and became a very important part of our team. He became someone we could all depend on as a kicker and a person. What you are about to read is Mike's journey, and how he has developed into an outstanding husband, father, and friend to many. If you can get one or two things out of this story to help you in your life, then Mike has attained his goal.

Coach Ron Labadie

    Adrian College Alumni

    Adrian College Hall of Fame

    Adrian College Head Football Coach

Forward

Feeling connected with a purpose is magic. Looking back to see the importance of these connections in your life is a true blessing. Writing the story of my experience in life, sports, and specifically football has made me appreciate all those who touched my life even more.

As I go through my life, I become more aware of how this life is truly like a highway. There are visions you see from peak mountaintops that can take your breath away and give you an emotional response that satisfies your soul. There are also views from valleys that can crush your spirit and make you wish for those mountaintops again. A successful journey uses a road map to guide you to your desired destination.

Yet, life does not provide a map giving us directions through our journey or a GPS. You would never go on a journey without planning the route to your destination. So how do you navigate life without a guide to keep you out of danger? I profess, faith influences your journey more than anything else.

Faith, family, and friends compose the details of the direction life can take and become. Faith in a higher power that has designed and directed our path in life connects us to our purpose. When I speak of family, I include blood relations—the family you were born into—along with those who come into your life who are so close they become part of your family. Friends may journey in and out of your life, but they can have a powerful impact on a season.

The stronger these pillars of faith, family, and friendships become, the richer life becomes. At some point, you look back and see the purpose revealed. Looking from this perspective, you see a reverse road map that shows you the interesting route you have taken.

This reverse road map becomes clearer to people at different times in their life, as mine is now to me. There is no way I would have taken this life path to get to this point, and if I were to try and plot it out myself, I would probably be lost on a dead-end road somewhere. Only divine guidance and intervention could have made my journey so successful.

So many times, I look back and ask, Why me? Why was I chosen to take this journey? The answer always becomes clearer because of God's great design and greater purpose: I was chosen. Humbling as this all has been, I am so grateful for the journey, the involvement, and my many friends and teammates. Without these connections and relationships, this story would not be possible.

I came into the world during the Cold War on January 6, 1964. Common to that era in our history, my mom stayed at home taking care of the home, me, and later my brother, John. My dad worked for the CIA/DIA at the National Photo Interpretation Center (NPIC) in a top-secret program developing aerial photo interpretation techniques to keep watch on enemies of our country. Maps were important in his job and played a key role in my upbringing.

My mid-1960s suburban upbringing was rather plain and standard. I led a rather nondescript life outside of Washington, DC, in the suburb of New Carrollton, Maryland. I was born in DC, born without a state (technically), though my alliances always swung to all things Maryland. The area's rich history in the origins of the US gave me pride about my roots.

Though some would deem my amazing story a supernatural success, I hope you will find the true scope of my success underlined with humility. The record-making success very few get to enjoy even for a brief time, let alone a lifetime, came through a confluence of circumstance, encouragement, and unexpected coaching and wisdom from standouts in the field as well as fellow players. So how does a guy from the suburbs of DC get the opportunity to become one of the most consistent placekickers in the history of NCAA Division III football history, and still, no one has heard about the achievements of the "Barefoot Kicker"?

First of all, I must admit, I did not achieve my accomplishments alone. I had many people around me throughout my life that played a role in my success. My faith, the true cornerstone of everything positive in my life, did not always receive my full recognition or appreciation. I know my faith's big picture, and I know without a doubt my security for the afterlife and who has guided my life to this point, but, like many, I feel I can grow yet stronger in my faith.

As I look back on my life, I was fortunate to be able to connect the dots to my youth growing up in New Carrollton. I grew up with a group of friends and neighbors who have truly become more like family over the years. There were about fifteen core kids in the neighborhood. Others came and went with families moving in and out of the neighborhood, but the long-term core people were key to grounding me and shaping early-life experiences. All the kids in the neighborhood—including Steve, Dave, Greg, and Robbie, who were my age—made quite a gathering for outdoor play, cookouts, and neighborhood gatherings back when neighbors gathered and interacted more regularly.

We had more fun than we probably should have had as a ragtag group of kids making memories determined to play for hours at a time—board games, creative out-of-doors games, and backyard pickup sports games.

In the winter, we made sled runs downhills in our yards and eventually through several connecting backyards fraught with danger and excitement. (I'm sure we would be shut down by some overarching social services department these days.) We dug tunnels in the dirt pile in our backyard of about ten feet in length that taught why projects underground really need special engineering—so they don't collapse and fall in on people. Ours did once, but we were able to get out safely with a healthy respect for miners for the future.

We attended events at the Capital Center in nearby Landover, Maryland, watching the Washington Bullets NBA team, Ringling Brothers Circus, Ice Capades, and many other major events. We attended baseball games at RFK Stadium to see the Washington Senators battle the Baltimore Orioles in the days of Frank Howard and Boog Powell before the Senators moved to Texas to become the Rangers. We even saw celebrities who stayed at the local Sheraton who had events at the Capital Center like Elvis, Muhammad Ali, and others. It was a good time to grow up, forming the deep bonds of friendship and family.

During the summer when we were twelve years old, we would walk about six blocks to the local drugstore to purchase baseball cards and come back to the neighborhood to trade and admire the different cards bought during each trip (all done without our parent's knowledge for fear they would say no). We would spend most of our days hanging out together until our parents called us home, usually by standing in the backyard and calling our name and the dreaded instruction, "Time to come home!" Who needed cell phones when you had this free calling plan?

I possessed many similar traits of firstborn children. I enjoyed the attention of my parents and tried to do the right things to stay in their good graces, with a driving sense of overachievement in all I tried. Shyness affected me greatly as a child. I'm not sure where it started or how it became such an issue for me at an early age. At different times in my life, it became paralyzing.

I imagine the anxiety was a result of trying to please others and to analyze any situation to understand what issues I might confront before I jumped in with both feet. I didn't want to fail— fail my family, my friends, myself, or God. Why I thought these things, I do not know. Maybe it was the way I was wired, or maybe it came from a competitive nature, but I wanted the best for everyone around me, not myself alone. I seemed to be preoccupied with how others were doing and always wanted the best for them, even before my own well-being.

I recall several instances when the seeds of shyness were sown, leading me to build emotional walls to isolate myself from outside pain. I remember a bus ride home one day where my next-door neighbor, Dave, and I were in the front of the bus talking. Dave said he knew of someone who liked me. I had my eye on one of the girls I thought was cute as well and hoped it was her. Dave asked who I thought it was, and I mentioned her name.

Dave began to laugh and said "Why would you think she would like you? There is no way she would ever like you." That's all I heard after that.

You see Dave was the lady's man of our group and a smooth operator with everyone. If he said something about girls, you listened. He also told me once that I was "lucky." How so? He said guys like you will only get better looking with age, but for people like himself, there is nowhere to go but to get uglier as they age. That stuck with me as well.

All I thought was, I can't wait until when I will be considered good looking, not that it would ever come. Luckily, he was wrong about that, as I have learned, and yes, he has aged well and is still a respectable good-looking guy with a good personality.

In fourth grade, my teacher was concerned about my quietness in class and discussed it with my parents at a parent/teacher conference. The teacher told my parents she was going to try to get me out of my shell and place the two most talkative students at desks on either side of me to help draw me out. The experiment didn't go as my teacher had expected. You see, the two talkative students suddenly became more like me, quiet and less disruptive to the class. So, ultimately, we all won I guess, and my strength to follow the rules and not talk during class was proven to be the right path.

Even this experience seemed to be a form of leadership I would learn and use throughout life. Honestly, it had more to do with my shyness and respect for the teachers. **I learned the life lesson to lead by example as well as focus, a key trait for kicking.** These traits would set up my future success as well.

Most of the time, I looked at relationships as an ever-elusive process that would always be my Achilles heel. My shyness would be the largest wall for me to scale to have a meaningful relationship with anyone new to my life, especially a person of the opposite sex. I was so shy, in fact, I would rarely speak the name of a female even if they were on friendly terms with me. When referring to females, I used pronouns like "her" or "she" rather than let anyone know I knew their name for fear they might think I liked a girl. This kept me from ridicule for desiring to have any type of relationship with a girl, even just a simple friendship.

Connections were difficult at times as well. Transitioning was a constant in my educational life. I transferred schools and school buildings throughout my elementary years from kindergarten onward. Only my relationships with the neighborhood friends remained stable and consistent. After first grade, I transitioned to a private Baptist school with my neighbor Dave, Riverdale Baptist School. The school transitioned through several buildings during our time at Riverdale Baptist until the final new build was made for the permanent home for sixth grade. Now a full-fledged K–12 school, the attendance grew each year. We had a soccer team I expected to play on when I got to high school, though that's a story for another book . . .

—1—
The Cornerstone

—1—
The Cornerstone

Faith is "the evidence of things not seen" (Hebrews 11:1). While I have never seen God, I truly believe he is real and ever-present in my life and truly has always been looking out for me. I was raised in a Christian home and attended church pretty much my whole life. I have attended multiple denominations where I found differences all along the spectrum from super-structured to some rather freewheeling beliefs.

The one constant I understood through them all was that God is omnipresent and omnipotent. Worship varies between denominations, and some are set in their ways with definite opinions about how to worship and how to get to heaven. I believe God has a different plan for each one of us. I believe God has a plan for us and helps guide us to fulfill his plan, but our free will and choices can take us closer to or further away from his master plan.

God's presence in my life is tied to my family in an amazingly and intricately woven tapestry of events. The story began before my birth when my Uncle Jimmy Lyons presided over the wedding vows of my parents. My uncle is, and will always be, a beacon of light that has guided my faith walk in so many ways. My uncle was instrumental in the development of the Presbyterian Church in America and one of the strongest Christian leaders I have known. Few can match Uncle Jimmy's gift of storytelling. He broke down the gospel as a demonstration of God's love and how we needed to serve others and walk in humble reverence as we serve.

In the early 1970s, Uncle Jimmy pastored a church in Swannanoa, North Carolina, just outside of Ashville. We visited several times throughout my childhood and always had a good time with my Aunt Phyllis and Uncle Jimmy. Phyllis was my mom's sister, and it fascinated me to hear stories they told about their upbringing in Holdenville, Oklahoma. I could always tell the love they had for one another and the importance of family to them both. The importance of a strong family bond was instilled deep in my soul even at a young age.

I always felt a special connection to Uncle Jimmy, and on one particular trip when I was around six, I became an unannounced partner in the church service. During that Sunday morning service, Uncle Jimmy had completed his sermon and was preparing to bless the congregation and greet the parishioners at the door as they left. I've been told that as Jimmy looked down from the pulpit at me sitting in the front of the church, he smiled, and nodded in recognition of my presence, as he did often.

Evidently, I took this signal as it was time for me to join him as he went to the door to greet the congregation. When he passed by my pew, I stood up as if it were planned and walked out beside him down the center aisle and stood with him. I helped him greet each person as they left the service, as any good associate pastor would do.

I don't remember much of this on my own, but my parents and Phyllis and Jimmy have reminded me over the years how professional and polished I acted and how it thrilled and impressed the congregation, who enjoyed my impromptu participation in their service. This is the first example I have of how God directed my actions and gave me the strength to squash anxiety of unfamiliar situations and people. I had a peace that told me I was safe with Uncle Jimmy and in God's house. When Jimmy was called home to heaven a few years ago, he left a legacy, and I'm sure he received a "well done good and faithful servant" when he arrived.

One's walk as a Christian can be like walking through a minefield of being strong in your beliefs and not wanting to make a mistake and have the world call you a hypocrite or fake. I have struggled with this double-edged sword for most of my life. My greatest positive strides have come when I let go of the control and fear of making a mistake, trusting God that my actions are in line with him and his plan for my life. The best part about giving up control is, when I follow that track, a pleasant and calming peace allows me to be more myself in challenging situations and comfortable with who I am.

Duckpin Bowling

One of the early organized group sports I participated in was a Saturday morning bowling league for duckpin bowling. A variation on the regular tenpin bowling most have seen on television, duckpin bowling uses a smaller ball—about five inches in diameter and about three and a half pounds in weight with no finger holes—and pins—about nine inches tall. It was just right for our nine-year-old size when the gang from the neighborhood began in the league.

Several years of our youth we headed off to the bowling alley and learned the fine art of rolling a clay ball about the size of our hand down the alley at half-size pins. It was great fun and something we all enjoyed participating in each week. This taught me how consistency and individual rituals contribute to success.

4

The whole gang participated in several sports throughout the years, sometimes on the same team and sometimes on separate teams. We bonded over little things like buying candy Pez dispensers, toys, and stickers from the vending machines as well as the thrill of winning games as teammates and rooting for each other to do well. Sportsmanship developed in our lives, and we were there for each other.

We also participated in several tournaments as individuals. I honestly didn't have a clue what the purpose of a tournament was at that age but knew I enjoyed bowling and my competitive spirit sought success. My inner voice always believed I was able to do better, and I pushed myself to be better each time I went out bowling. During some of these tournaments, I accomplished some winning ways and was awarded a trophy for placing first in the region in my age group, my first outside athletic recognition. I must admit, I enjoyed the feeling it gave me, but I made sure to keep those feelings to myself. Though a bit naive in many aspects of the tournament and life in general, I did enjoy this feeling of winning.

BACKYARD SPORTS

Some of the greatest memories of my early childhood were the backyard pickup games we played in various yards. We played football, Wiffle ball, high jump pit, bike rodeo, and any games needing a flat surface in the Lambs' yard at the bottom of the hill. There were permanent bare spots in the yard from all the activities we had there.

We had a kickball field painted on the street around the corner for all to enjoy. Kicking balls became one of my favorite activities. I would visualize kicking techniques like others visualized being the star quarterback or receiver.

My first memory of kicking and football was in the Lambs' backyard, and I always wanted to be like the Redskin's kick-er-punter team, Mark Moseley and Mike Bragg, back in the '70s and '80s. Nothing beats the dream of playing in the NFL one day. I honestly never thought I could make the NFL and set my sights on professional soccer, but it would be a good fallback in case I didn't make the soccer dream come true.

I was given the duty of kicking off to the other team. The Lambs' had a good-sized yard with room for our crew of 11- and 12-year-olds to play. I specifically remember thinking I was making my professional debut on one kickoff. I saw myself physically making the motions; I visualized the kick before the play. I hadn't done that consciously before, but I distinctly remember doing it that time.

When my foot contacted the ball, it sailed perfectly from one end of the Lambs' yard over the fence to the next yard, over the weeping willow tree, and over the next fence into the next yard! No one had ever done that before. We all began to cheer, and I'm sure I had a sheepishly dumbfounded look on my face as we celebrated the kick.

Someone had to go out of the gate and walk around the block to the other house to retrieve the ball from the other yard. I don't remember much more about the game that day, but I do remember **that was my first inkling I wanted to kick a football, and I wanted my friends to join in any celebrations that may come with it.**

Another kick worth noting happened not long after during a street kickball game. We were split up into teams, and I had a turn to kick. I remember making full contact with the ball, which sailed off my foot and went high into the air. It traveled across the diamond and over everyone's head and landed in the neighbor's backyard, farther than anyone had kicked a ball before.

Again, hearing the excited cheers and adulations, I felt a real sense of accomplishment over that kick. . . until we noticed the ball was square in the mouth of the neighbor's dog. He had punctured a hole in the side of the ball, and we were done for the day. Feeling terrible about the ball took some of the air out of my celebration. **I learned that day, don't get too high and don't get too low in your celebrations.**

— 2 —
Sporting Dreams

— 2 —
Sporting Dreams

As the New Carrollton group grew older, the Boys and Girls Club began to gain more of our attention as we dreamt of becoming the next great sports legend. We went through basketball, baseball, track, and soccer. These sports began to feed our dreams and separate those who had natural talent from the wannabes. Steve was far and away the purest natural athlete of our group and good at most every sport he tried. Dave and Greg, coordinated and good-sized for our age, excelled at several sports including basketball and soccer.

I, on the other hand, had to work hard to get any success or awaken any latent abilities. I didn't even last one session in track. I was so unconditioned I couldn't even make it through the practice sessions, too out of shape to run the routines. I always believed I was fast, but reality showed me how slow I was.

I also didn't have the mental strength that was needed to compete. I eventually realized the mental aspects of sports correlate greatly with the success I wanted to achieve. If your heart's not into what you are doing, you will not achieve your full potential.

In baseball, I was a terror at the plate, or better yet I was filled with terror at the plate! I didn't come up through the ranks of T-ball and coach's pitch. Instead, I jumped right into the mix with good ol'-fashioned kid pitch. The first practice of my first year, it was my turn up for batting practice. Mind you, I had never swung a bat or played anything other than Wiffle ball in the back yard with the guys. I took a few swings and missed by a mile each time. The coach kept encouraging me to keep my eye on the ball.

The guy pitching looked more like a minor league pitcher in size compared to me. He asked the coach if it was ok for him to "really throw one hard at the plate." The coach knew the power the pitcher had from previous seasons and agreed for him to fire one across the plate.

Imagine, if you will, a frightened boy with a wooden stick in his hand wanting desperately to look respectable to these new teammates and "stand in there" for this pitch. This was our first practice, and the coach hadn't received any protective equipment, including batting helmets for the team. I was standing there hoping I wouldn't look too silly when this real pitch came across the plate. I thought, that's how it looked when the pros did it, and they always had good control.

The pitcher reared back and let one go at a velocity that had to be over fifty miles-per-hour. I stood in there like a trooper until contact was made. Not with the bat, but with the side of my head! I went down in a heap. Everyone rushed in to see how I was. The pitcher apologized profusely. The coach asked how I felt. I was pretty out of it, and all I could think was, don't cry. I rubbed my head until the pain subsided and kept my eyes closed and sat behind the fence until it was time to go home. "Why me" was all I could think.,

I stuck it out that year, usually playing in left field so I couldn't do much harm to the team. I wasn't very good and didn't have a strong arm, nor was I very accurate with my throws. I did make one throw late in the year when I got to a ball that was finally hit near me. My coach praised me for what an awesome throw I made as if it were instinct to throw to the right base and hold the runners. I remember I got to the ball as it rolled toward me, picked it up, and just threw it as hard as I could at one of my teammates so they could make a play and keep us in the game. I just happened to throw to the right guy. Honestly, I got lucky.

Throughout the year, I made sure when I was at bat to have the helmet on. A false sense of security boded well for my style of play. I struck out quite a bit, but I also walked quite a bit. The coach said he was amazed how I would shrink myself down in my stance (I imagine it now more like the fetal position). The pitchers, intimidated to throw accurately, often ended up walking me.

Again, I didn't have a clue what I was doing, and it was all divine intervention I didn't get killed! It all paid off in the end as our team took first place in our age bracket, and I ended up receiving a trophy. The trophy made me feel pretty good, and I even felt a spark of **"Why Not Me?"** beginning to burn.

I felt so good I went out the next year again, and this time I wanted to be the catcher. This was the generation of Johnny Bench and the Big Red Machine, and I figured with all the protective gear a catcher has, I would stay safe and not do much harm to the team. (When you don't know something about a position, don't try to bluff your way through!)

My batting didn't improve much from the previous year, but I did manage to hit a home run during the season. But we did not win at the same pace as the previous year, And to add insult to injury, I got injured.

Did I mention I didn't know what I was doing? I saw Johnny Bench make some amazing plays on television like tagging people out at home plate. I got my chance one day and received a ball from the infielder in plenty of time to tag the runner coming in from third. I turned and blocked the plate, trying to look the part, holding the catcher's mitt out in front of me to make the tag. No one told me about the force of collisions and how you need to keep your fingers protected and not pointing straight out. Needless to say, a violent collision took place, and I ended up with two fractured fingers on my left hand in the catcher's mitt and dropped the ball, so the runner ended up being safe. Again, "Why Me?" Not a shining moment in my athletic career, but it was my last game of organized baseball, playing in fear for my life! **What I did take away from this experience is that by giving your all and trying to improve, you will make progress. Keep a positive outlook and you can do amazing things.**

Soccer was next up, and I had a good feeling about this sport. It was a growing sport at the time, and there were not too many ways to get majorly hurt. Without a lot of dominant players in the area, it was a good team sport that seemed like it could be fun. This is where my dream began. In my first year of playing soccer, my team had some good individual players on it, including my neighbor Dave. A great coach taught us the basics and made us into a real team. So good, in fact, that we ran the season with an undefeated record!

The year was good overall, but I do remember a few times when I was teased about my weight. My portly frame fed self-esteem issues for sure. Around my neighborhood friends, I didn't see or feel any of the drawbacks or shortcomings. Meeting new kids who didn't have filters awakened me to a new dynamic. At times it hurt, and I buried my feelings, trying not to let them see how they bothered me. I wasn't always successful, and when my face showed some pain, they attacked aggressively.

Dave would deflect and stand up for me when he noticed teasing, but a few knew just how to drive the comments home in passing. I was able to channel that pain into strong defense that my coach noticed. Not many got around to take shots on our goal. This positive reinforcement pushed my desire to become better and work on strengthening my kicking leg. Then I could turn the other team away from our end of the field. I secretly wanted to get strong enough to kick from one end of the field to the other and score a goal. The feeling I got from playing soccer was the best I had ever felt, and I knew I was going to play professional soccer when I grew up!

The next soccer season, I was fortunate enough to make the county's B soccer team. There was an A team and a B team. My coach from last year was the county B team coach, and he hand-picked athletes from the intramural participants in our age group. Dave, me, and many other players from the last team were chosen . We added some additional great players and proceeded to dominate the other teams from the county.

We went undefeated again! We received a letter and a trophy for our efforts, and I knew from that experience that this would bring me out of my shell and give me the confidence to succeed in life. **Work hard and you will be rewarded!** I couldn't wait for next year.

— 3 —
Neighborhood Antics

— 3 —
Neighborhood Antics

One Christmas, my friend Steve and I each got wooden go-kart kits. Our dads helped us—well, it's more like we tried to help them—build these homemade non-motorized go-karts out of wood. We had the most amazing hill we rode them down . . . while pressing a chunk of tire nailed to a piece of 1x2 for the brake. Then we pushed the carts back up the hill to do it all over again. This lasted for a couple of years before the wood began to rot and the carts naturally fell apart.

One day we had a creative idea to make a super cart, and we took Steve's cart parts and constructed a double cart using some spare wood from another of his dad's home projects. We were the MacGyvers (the original Richard Dean Anderson version) of the time and excited about our accomplishment, so excited, Steve and I recruited our brothers to test the new configuration down the opposite side of the block with a smaller incline. Our brothers were four and five years younger than us and less experienced in the art of go-kart driving than we were, but they were game.

After giving them a quick lesson on steering and staying out of the way of any cars, we gave their cart a push down the hill. They began screaming almost immediately, and we started laughing at the antics. We yelled for them to turn away from the curb, but to no avail, they crashed into a storm drain and damaged the newly designed dual cart we spent so much time perfecting. Evidently, the steering wasn't as taut as it needed to be, and they also discovered there wasn't a brake for the cart, so they didn't have much of a chance. But it was one hilarious ten-second ride!

All summer, we kept cool at the local community pool a few blocks from our neighborhood. We had yearly passes there, where we all learned how to swim. Once we passed our swim test, we were able to swim in any part of the pool without parental supervision.

Our parents allowed us to walk to the pool with the neighbors and hang out for hours on end. Again . . . a different time. Between Memorial Day and Labor Day, they blasted the hits over a speaker system only silenced by the hourly reminder for those under eighteen to leave the pool for a rest break. I'm not sure if it was for us kids to rest or to give the lifeguards a rest from all our chaos and fun.

I remember the year I tried diving in the twelve-foot depth, a big step up for any kid at the time. They had a low board and a high dive, which to a preteen looked to be about fifty feet high. I conquered it during my last season there. I still felt queasy every time I went up the ladder but to avoid the sheer embarrassment of walking back down in shame, I braved it out.

It took a while to learn how to dive and not get a nose full of chlorinated pool flushing my sinuses. **That summer I learned how to talk myself through anxieties with internal drive, a good tool I would later draw upon to keep my attention focused any time I needed for the task before me.**

Intellectually, we challenged each other through board games. There were the typical board games like Monopoly, Stratego, Battleship, King Oil, and the king of all games, Risk! This game lasted for hours at a time and usually ended up with Robbie winning with his superior intelligence. He was our real-life neighborhood rocket scientist who went on to achieve great academic success and became a physics professor at a university.

All those hours of gamesmanship taught us valuable lessons in strategy and visualizing success, even if we were at a disadvantage. I learned to respect other players, their talents, strategic thought process, and attention to detail. These additional skills eventually formed the basis for critical and strategic thinking I would use in my preparing for a kick and improving my game. I learned many skills in Maryland that came to mean so much to me and my development as a person.

Life was good in our neighborhood, and I felt safe and secure among my friends.

18

— 4 —
Changes

— 4 —
Changes

Then life changed on a dime. My Dad decided to retire from his government position as a photo interpreter for the DIA/CIA. He took an early-out and retired at forty-five. That alone was not a bad thing, as I noticed how my dad's work took a toll on him physically and mentally. It was a very stressful job.

I didn't know all the details at that time in my life, but what came out over the years clarified so much. Dad was a part of the intelligence community that tracked enemies of the state and had the responsibility of confirming compliance with the SALT II Nuclear Treaty with our Cold-War foe, then called the USSR.

The dagger to the heart was the next step: we were going to move! Either to South Texas almost to the border of Mexico or to the unknown land of mid-Michigan. At thirteen, this was the absolute worst news I could have imagined. I was about to leave everyone and everything I had ever known for something new. To an overly shy introvert, this felt like a death sentence.

I didn't know what I was going to do. I would not get to play on the Riverdale Baptist High School soccer team! Do these areas have a soccer program? Will there be kids my age in the neighborhood I will get to know as well as my group in New Carrollton? A resounding **"Why Me?"** rose from the depths of my soul and roared throughout my brain.

After months of speculation, it was decided we would move to a small town in Michigan and Dad would help his stepfather run his air pollution control business. We would be moving to Fenton, Michigan, a little town south of Flint and north of Detroit. All I knew was life was going to be cold and dark—for the rest of my life.

Michigan and a New Life

My mind was a fertile little thing, and I was convinced I would not find anyone like the crew I grew up and hung out with in New Carrollton, Maryland. I didn't give life in Michigan much of a chance. I was right, of course, about the friends in Maryland, but I did survive, barely.

We had nice enough neighbors and even some extremely pretty neighbors next door I envisioned getting to know as we moved into our new house. Actually, I was crazy thinking any girl would want to hang out with me right then with my emotional state of mind. Mom even chided me to go over and say hi when we got settled in, but my shyness reared its ugly head, and I just turned red and started unpacking.

There were many developments in my life when we first moved to Fenton. This was a General Motors town with many employed by the auto industry plants in Flint or related supply businesses in the area. These people were down to earth and had strong wills, something I lacked at the time. I was an extremely naive teenager who desperately believed I had it together, as so many do at that age.

I became more introverted and built taller and thicker protective walls around my emotions. I didn't want to be here and didn't want anyone to find out how lonely I was. All I wanted to do was to somehow get back to New Carrollton and be with my friends again.

We lived behind the middle school, so I had a quick walk around the fence to get on the school property. I remember going into the eighth grade and not knowing anyone. I only knew my neighbor by sight. Being the new kid made me a fascination for some.

I didn't speak the "language" too well either. I didn't realize it at the time, until one day the science teacher asked a question to which I knew the answer. I raised my hand and answered "What liquid is filled with carbonation?" correctly, "soda pop." But the class erupted in laughter, and the teacher chuckled as well and said, "That is right, but we just call it pop around here." I'm sure I turned three shades of red and smiled, realizing trying to fit in would make this a difficult year.

I remember early in eighth grade we went on a class field trip to the movie theater to see the original, first *Star Wars* (now renamed *A New Hope*). This is pretty awesome, I thought. I made my way to a seat and there were a couple of girls sitting behind me giggling and talking. I felt special when they tapped me on the shoulder to ask me a question. "Hey, can you say something? You have a funny accent."

"What do you want me to say?" They just giggled and sat back in their seat as the lights began to dim and the movie was starting. I slumped a little lower in my seat, ashamed to have thought a cute girl would think anything positive of me. I enjoyed the movie, only because I had seen it with my friends in Maryland and remembered the good time we had watching it together.

Bullies have been around for years. I had never experienced being a target since I usually had an ability to blend into the background successfully. This changed in eighth grade, and I was targeted by an individual who for some reason wanted to physically beat me up. He challenged me multiple times to meet him outside after school where he said he would beat me up. Why? I honestly do not know. Perhaps he was jealous of things I brought to the school or felt threatened by my presence or he just didn't like me and decided to beat me up so that he can look better to his friends.

I always got nervous towards the end of the day and tried to beat him out of the school so he wouldn't have an opportunity to act on his threats. I took the nonviolent approach, avoiding an altercation with him. Eventually into the second semester, the chiding stopped, and he left me alone. Not letting others influence me to change who I was turned out to be a quality that would benefit me more later in life. Though, I know it might have been more—a supernatural gift from a guardian angel that kept me safe on many occasions.

Scouting Outlet

I found a Boy Scout troop through our church and continued a scouting career I began in Maryland. Scouting became a sanctuary for me during much of my teen years. Our troop was active in high-adventure activities, even beyond the usual council activities. Our troop took summer camps to some of the best places outside of the scout camps, and there were many ways we developed as scouts and individuals.

One of the best summer camps I recall was a trip to the Catoctin Mountains in western Maryland. Not only was this exciting for me to be able to go back to Maryland, but we were going to be camping and repelling near Camp David, the presidential retreat. We arrived after a long car ride from Fenton and needed to stretch our legs. I had been to this area before the move with a troop I was involved with in New Carrollton.

I had a vague remembrance of a trail we could take and see the gates for Camp David, and the troop leaders thought it would be good to stretch our legs before we set up camp so off we went. It wasn't too far, and we hiked up a couple of hills and came to a fence offset in the woods.

My faint memory was rewarded with a gate further up and a sign marking Camp David. At that time, President Carter was involved in talks with the Israeli and Egyptian prime ministers for a Mideast peace treaty. We thought how nice it would be if they were all going to be here for more discussions and we could somehow see them.

Our troop numbered about twenty-five for that trip plus five adult leaders. We had quite a gathering on the roadside about 150 feet from the actual gate and barbed wire fence. We could see several guards at the front gate, including a jeep with a machine gun mounted on the back for security. There was a swinging wooden arm to stop vehicles at the gate before entry and additional security items around the grounds. One particular natural-looking item was a laser eye hidden in a stand disguised as a birdhouse. The older scout leaders noticed this and told the younger scouts to stay to the back of that box and not break the beam.

One would think that would be enough for some of the scouts to stay back and respect the safety features. But, unfortunately, that warning triggered one scout to look for himself. He walked over to the box, stuck his head squarely in front of the opening, and made the announcement to the rest of the troop, "Yep, that is a beam in there!"

Almost immediately there was activity at the gate. All the

scouts began to get excited something was about to happen. Could it be that the president was about to show up for more peace talks between the Israelis and Egyptians? The older scouts began to gather the younger scouts together and told everyone to settle down and pay attention. We could see several additional guards appear, and many had binoculars looking back at us! Another guard stepped up into the back of the jeep and manned a large machine gun which now pointed in our direction. Something big was about to happen!

Suddenly a green National Park Service station wagon roared its engine as it drove quickly up the hill toward us. The ranger had his window down and began to flag us down as he gave a stern command, "You need to vacate this area! You are not supposed to be up here! Didn't you see the signs? No standing, stopping or loitering is allowed here!"

The troop leadership took heed and began to guide us back down the hill to our campsite. The nice guards at the camp escorted us along the fence line until we were out of sight, all the while keeping their binoculars and mounted machine guns trained on our position. I can only imagine their discussions that night regarding our incursion!

As luck would have it, marching down the hill revealed the signs denoting "No stopping, standing or loitering" located along the hill. The problem was, they all faced the opposite direction we had hiked up the hill, so we honestly never saw them, or we wouldn't have had machine guns trained on us! The rest of our trip didn't have as much excitement as that first day, but we enjoyed several days filled with hiking and rappelling down some of the cliffs we were able to climb.

Another summer camp we travelled to Fort Knox, Mammoth Caves, and King's Island amusement park in the Northern Kentucky/Southern Ohio area. Camp holds special memories in my life, and I was lucky enough to have my dad be part of all of them as well. When we went to Fort Knox, Dad was able to share some special memories of where he had to learn the look of the tank tracks left on the ground and develop additional techniques for his photo interpretation work with NPIC. This aided his analysis of reconnaissance photos from U-2 high-altitude planes and satellites around the world. Little stories like this made me appreciate some of the trials Dad had to go through with his job. His responsibilities were so secretive, he was not able to leave the country for at least four years after his retirement for fear of foreign governments kidnapping him to try to coerce information from him.

Dad also had an adventurous side as he tried to keep up with the scouts during our day trip to King's Island. He always carried the prized camera he had used for years during his missions for NPIC to take pictures for the troop during our outings. He once leaned out of a helicopter in Southeast Asia for a photo interpretation key during the Vietnam conflict.

When we rode "The Beast," one of the fastest roller coasters of the time, Dad enjoyed it, but one of the screws that held the camera to the case vibrated out and fell. After he laughed off losing the screw for his camera, all he could talk about was how exhilarating the ride was, taking it two more times that day. His easy-going personality about something that meant so much to him showed me a side of a personality that was in me through DNA, **don't get too high or too low with your emotions—integrity matters**. This emotional state would guide me and direct my future success in life more than I could know.

My journey in scouts concluded with the achievement of the rank of Eagle. The journey was a long and winding road that my parents probably wondered if I would ever complete. I felt immense pride to achieve the rank, honored to be in a class of people like my cousin Tony Steve, the eldest son of my Uncle Jimmy and Aunt Phyllis. All my life I heard the stories of Tony Steve and his brother Phillip. Tony had achieved his Eagle rank at a young age by showing dedication and focus on details to achieve his goal.

I remember wanting to duplicate his efforts and one day be a member of this scouting elite, an achievement that only four percent of scouts have achieved since the inception of scouting in the US. The achievement of Eagle Scout also helped my self-confidence and allowed me to grow as a person and hold myself a little more confidently knowing I had achieved something few would realize. Being an Eagle would later assist me in securing at least two of my jobs in the business world as the interviewers gave me the nod over other candidates due to this achievement.

Character development, confidence building, camaraderie, and the brotherhood of individuals working together for a common purpose are some of the traits my time in the scouts developed. Identifying with a group working toward a common purpose would become a building block for my athletic future and future success in life.

— 5 —
New Hometown Disappointments and Successes

— 5 —
New Hometown Disappointments and Successes

I didn't know much of the Fenton area or how to get involved in many of the things for people my age. It was too late for me to try out for the football team, and I hadn't heard about any soccer programs. In reality, soccer hadn't made it to mid-Michigan at the time. It was truly a football and basketball town.

I tried out for the basketball team in the fall of eighth grade and made it. The coach saw something in my determination and effort. Admittedly, I did not have the skill many on the team had nor the height to be a force, but I did have the right attitude. I remember working hard during practice and leaving everything on the court, which would help me throughout life and my sports career. At the end of the year, I remember scoring a few points and playing in several games in a mop-up role (a third-string starter as it were).

One game in particular I remember playing had gotten out of hand in our favor, and the coach allowed the team manager to play. That guy ended up scoring more points in one game than I did all season. I had never much felt like I was part of the team, and this led to a few swipes from teammates saying they should have kept the manager on the team and left me off. (He was their friend, and I was the new guy.) **Kind of crushing to the ego, but that showed me I had to work harder during practice and be the best I could be.**

It was an exhausting year, but the season proved I had the internal desire to do what it takes to better myself, no matter the circumstances that were presented. The coach's praise for my attitude and hard work during practice throughout the season fueled my desire to do my best in any practice situation.

FOOTBALL CAREER

Sportswise, next up was ninth-grade football. This was it. What I had been waiting for. Summer voluntary weight training was about to start, and it was where I could come out of my shell. The first night of voluntary conditioning, I had my mom drive me to the high school. As we sat in the parking lot, I froze. I didn't see anyone I knew, and a strange paralyzing fear come over me. What if they already had a kicker/punter? What if there was competition for the position I wanted? Would I be good enough? Strong enough? Or am I just going to embarrass myself? I didn't have the answers, and I didn't want to find out. I told my mom to take me home. I didn't want to go in.

She did her best to talk me into going. I resisted to the point I broke down in the car. I was not ready to do this. Who did I think I was? We left, and I had serious doubts about my character and my true desire to play football on a team. To her credit, Mom never pushed me and just supported me through my meltdown. She knew it was something I had to work through and come to my own resolution.

A couple of weeks later, the mandatory practice began, and I pulled myself together to give it a try. I was still nervous and scared as you-know-what, but I knew I had to go in order to make the team. The coaches asked what position each athlete wanted to play. I of course said punter/kicker. They said great, but what position on offense and defense.

I didn't know how any of these other positions worked, and I was sure I would get killed trying any other position other than kicker. So, I shrugged my shoulders and gave a look like the clueless kid I was, and they said how about the offensive line and linebacker? "Ok" squeaked from my voice, and with that, my football career began.

I'll be honest, I did not excel learning the plays and assignments when I had never played organized football in my life. I again found my place as a third-string starter, and that was only because we only had enough players for three teams. I was clueless, and I'm sure the coaches could see that.

To top all that, I had competition at placekicker from a guy on the team that had a cannon for a leg, Mark, and could kick the ball like there was no tomorrow. My saving grace was his slightly inconsistent accuracy. The coaches must have seen something in me when I kicked. Resigned to the fact I was not going to make improvements to become an effective offensive lineman or a linebacker, they sent me to the other field with some footballs to work on my kicking.

Was I being separated from the players or given my opportunity of a lifetime to improve in the one thing I did have a passion for? I didn't care about the separation part. I was alone to improve on my passion, and I knew how to take it from there. I'd set the footballs on the kicking tee and kick them up and down the other practice field, working on technique and accuracy. By the end of the year, I was getting better and ended as the starting kicker for extra points. We didn't have much need for field goals because the team was so dominant; when they were close enough, we scored touchdowns. We went undefeated for the year and truly overwhelmed our opponents.

Sophomore year was much the same, only the coaches started me out kicking by myself and working on my technique. I was entrenched as the first-string kicker for extra points and field goals while Mark continued with the kickoffs. The team dominated again, going undefeated that year.

In one game, an extra-point try went badly: the ball was hiked over the head of the holder. I remember pure panic consuming my brain, and, as if by instinct, I turned and ran after the ball. I had no business going after the ball in the first place and no clue what to do if I did recover the ball. We never practiced this scenario.

I remember getting to the ball first and scooping it up. Next, I saw a mass of players moving in so many directions, and I had to find one with the same color jersey! Luckily, I spotted one and threw the ball to him. It was our tight end, Paul, who ran back toward my position on the field. The miracle of the whole play was that he was a legal receiver, so I had my first, and only, pass attempt as a completion. Granted, it ended up being for negative yardage, but it was a successful play, and Paul made me look like I knew what I was doing. Not sure if I ever conveyed it, but thanks, Paul!

I enjoyed much success and an amazing surprise toward the end of the season. Along with Paul, our starting linebacker and my target for the crazy extra-point play, I was pulled up to the varsity for the final three games! The rumor mill conveyed that moving up to the varsity hadn't been done for many years at our high school. There had been an injury to a starter who happened to be the first-team kicker, linebacker, and running back, and they needed some help to stay in the chase for a league championship.

It was such a surreal experience — nothing this spectacular happens to me. **Why me?**

In the first game, we won fairly easily, and I made all my extra-point attempts. The second game was homecoming, and we exploded for seven touchdowns. After making all my attempts that day too, I was on cloud nine.

The final game was the clincher: we win, and we are league champs. We ended up losing the hard-fought game, and, worse yet, I had missed an extra point. I felt terrible for the team and as if the loss was all my fault, that I let them down.

Luckily, one of the seniors at the time, Greg—who I also knew through Scouts—came up to me and gave me a pep talk I will always remember. He said "It wasn't your fault; we didn't play up to our potential. Mistakes were made by many people. We appreciate what you have done over the last couple of weeks to help us get to this point. Keep your head up, keep working at it, and you'll do fine."

This talk meant so much and turned my mood around. I held my head a little higher knowing I did contribute over the last few weeks. I just felt bad and wanted the championship for them. That day I learned another piece of my foundation: what to do when things don't go my way in life.

Junior year was going to be the most memorable. I had come off the three-game stint on the varsity the previous year, boosting my confidence. Increased accuracy and leg strength gave the varsity coaches confidence in me as well.

The year was one of disappointment as a team though. After blasting away the competition in the previous two years, our team experienced a significant loss for the first time as a team. After being defeated in two games, we didn't win the league championship as expected.

I was awarded first-team All-Metro League status as a place-kicker, which came truly a surprise for me as it was the first individual recognition I had earned. Honored by the distinction, I became hungry for this type of positive affirmation in the future. I knew this was awarded only after great thought and debate. If I wanted to receive it again, I had to work hard the following year. I knew my next step: to work on my mental aspect during the off-season.

MICHIGAN KICKING SCHOOL

By the end of my junior year, my coach suggested I attend the University of Michigan Kicking School. No matter your feelings about the team or university, kicking in the "Big House" adds some excitement that would naturally intimidate anyone. I was going to make my stand here and show the college coaches I was worthy of a scholarship offer after they saw my kicking abilities.

As fate would have it, there were many good kickers there that day. Those who had done this training before were better prepared than others. I honestly didn't have a clue what to expect. Many had a water bottle—not me. Many had special shoes—not me. Many knew what was coming and could mentally prepare for it—not me. Don't get me wrong, I did pick up some key pointers on steps and follow-through and upped my game a little that day, but I was more interested in how this was going to move *my* plans forward.

The time came at the end of camp to have a little fun and show off our abilities. They were going to start us out at an extra point and move us back five yards per round as kind of a round-robin tournament. When you miss, you are out and get to watch the rest. I had a quiet reserve about me and figured I'd make it at least to a 40- or 45-yard field goal.

The first round began, and the anticipation began to rise. There were several who had some serious skills and kicked like they were ready to go to the next level. There were even a few who missed the extra point range. Can you believe it? Extra-point range is only a 20-yard field goal. I secretly thought, I'm glad that isn't me—that would be embarrassing!

It was finally my turn. I thought, 'the coaches had better dust off their offer sheet and add my name to the list after this one with confidence in my abilities'. I became a little nervous with all eyes on me, and feeling the pressure and going too deep into my head. Then all I could think was, don't miss! Mentally, I approached the ball, kicked, and looked up to see it sail majestically over the netting behind the uprights . . . Reality afforded me a different view as the ball hit squarely on the crossbar and bounced back to the field! I was right—that was embarrassing!

I was devastated and distraught. How would the coaches know what they were missing out on? How would I get my chance to show them I can do this? . . . Well, the short answer is, I would not. The day was over, and I was relegated to watching from the sidelines as the kicks progressed and the rest of the players eventually joined me.

What I learned that day would prove more valuable to me later. I had selfishly approached this camp as a day all about me. *My* abilities. *My* skills. *My* worthiness to be recruited to a major Division I program. The experience knocked me down a block or two off my pedestal. **When your attitude revolves around you, the very things you desire most won't go your way.** What a valuable lesson!

P.S. I vowed I'd do what I could to be the best at kicking extra points from now on. . . . If I only knew how powerful that memory would be.

— 6 —
Grasping at Glory

— 6 —
Grasping at Glory

Senior year arrived, and everyone held high expectations for our team, as I did for myself. Coming off a rather disappointing kicking camp and I knew I would only have this season to make a positive impression on college recruiters and earn a football scholarship.

I worked hard throughout the year on my technique and accuracy during my solitary practice sessions. I would practice by myself and come over to the team at the end of practice. Some days they would run game-situation drills and have me come in for a field-goal attempt. Most days, I would join the team for sprints at the end of practice before going home. My competitive nature pushed me to try and finish in the top tier of sprinters each time. Not easy, but fulfilling.

Early in the year, we had a surprise visit from the placekicker for the Detroit Lions, Eddie Murray. Eddie was early in his career at the time and known for being an accurate kicker and an All-Pro during his rookie season. He came to Fenton to make a special appearance at the opening of a new business in town, and the owner made it possible for him to stop by our practice and give the kickers some pointers. I had never met a professional kicker and remember his demeanor as very pleasant and humble.

Murray wanted to look at my kicking style and give me some pointers. He told me he didn't have much to say about my technique and was impressed with my discipline of practicing on my own during practice. I remember he suggested I be careful as to the number of kicks I make during the week and be sure to lower the number of kicks closer to game day. Logical and good advice I just needed to put into practice. He also observed I was using a two-inch-block tee to kick my extra points and field goals. The nice high block allowed me to add some height on the ball and be sure to clear the line and avoid defensive blocks.

Eddie suggested I use a one-inch-block tee. He offered this would make an easier transition if I had intentions of moving forward in my kicking career. This single suggestion would be a key factor at the end of my collegiate kicking career, more than anyone could ever foresee!

I remember he was generous with his time and stayed around to talk to some of the other guys after practice as well. Eddie stopped by my locker and out of the blue asked my shoe size. Honestly, I had no clue of my own shoe size at the time, so I blurted out a size. Eddie said, "That's too bad. I have some used shoes I would send over to you. They send me a bunch of shoes and they are like new." It turned out, I said a half size too big, so he thought they wouldn't fit. Hard lesson on my part. Look into your own shoe first, and get the right size.

As it was, I wore the exact same size as Eddie Murray and could have had several of his used cleats he got straight from the manufacturer! Lesson learned! Perhaps I didn't need the shoes anyway, or maybe it would help me, contributing to a future "barefoot" mentality? As the year went on, I transitioned to the one-inch tee for my future, and the transition was relatively seamless.

As seniors, we expected this to be the year that we would reassert ourselves as the power we were my first two years in the league. But our team experienced disappointment early in the season and began to fall apart. The low point of the year came when we ended up losing to a team that had the longest losing streak in the state at the time. I have no recollection as to why we lost, I just knew we didn't play as a team, and the opponent played the game of their lives.

The pain of that loss stung. We kept the score close at the end, and it came down to an onside kick. If we got control, we'd have had a chance to score and win the game. If not, the game was over since we were out of time-outs and they could run the clock out. I lined up for the kick and prayed I'd make the perfect kick. I had not practiced this type of kick much. Quite frankly, we were always so dominant, it wasn't used much the previous three years. The kick was unsuccessful, and we ended up losing the game.

I took the loss personally as my last kick didn't get the job done. I remember looking for excuses and reasons for the loss, but it always came back to my kick. Though it had been an opportunity to become a hero, I had to reconcile my efforts were not the sole reason for the loss.

Tracy, a friend, spoke to me after the game to try and bring me out of my dejection and disappointment. Looking back on that conversation, I should have appreciated her positive attitude more, but I had built a wall, and the self-pity party was raging inside. The bottom line my friend pointed out was that this was a team sport and a team loss. If others would have played to their potential, there was no way we would have been in such a close game. Many people had issues that day, and we didn't play as a team.

Mercifully, the end of the season came, yet I was disappointed I didn't make the All-League team. I understood this wasn't going to bode well for my chances of landing a Division I scholarship. The end-of-the-year banquet did provide some hope for the future, though. At this, the coaches would give a synopsis of the previous season, ending with awards.

The big football award was the Guy Bateman Award, given to the player who the coaches deemed the hardest and most dedicated worker during the year. I always believed this award went to the best athlete or the best player on the team, like an MVP. I listened to the things the coaches were saying and thought this guy had to be one of their favorites, but I couldn't figure out who it was. They said a name, but it didn't register with me at first. The guys sitting around me started clapping and told me, "Go up there"; they called my name!

I shook the cobwebs out of my head in disbelief and basically floated up to receive the trophy. I do not remember anything about the experience. . . . I was in total disbelief. I remember the coach saying they needed the trophy back to get my name engraved on it. I took it back up after showing my parents and the guys I was sitting with, and the coach told my parents how impressed they were with my work ethic. Though the coaches did not know enough about kicking to help me much, I worked hard. It all paid off, as my effort had made me a good kicker. The Guy Bateman Award was a great honor and made me believe I had something special to offer a college at the next level.

— 7 —
High School Hang-Ups

— 7 —
High School Hang-Ups

High school itself was more of a minefield of opportunities both missed and discovered. I settled into my routine and was quite the accomplished wallflower. I desperately wanted to engage and do the typical things teens are portrayed doing in the movies, but I was also awkward socially—in action and words. Though I had friends, I never felt the same connection I had with the gang from Maryland. Because most of the Fenton students had grown up together and known each other for life in this small town. I was an outsider, or at least I believed myself to be.

As I look back now, my self-consciousness and worry about what others would think of me and my actions caused me to never let my real self out there for others to accept. I took the wrong approach, and if I knew then what I know now, I'd have changed things sooner. Life is so much better when you live to lift and help others rather than worrying about what others will think which will paralyze your actions.

Some of the most interesting out-of-the-box opportunities happened in French class. I had a teacher who was truly passionate about the language and teaching it to her students. She taught us the French national anthem, the intricacies of the language as detailed as our regular English class, and some performance art that was the essence of the French language.

I enjoyed the class, but there seemed to be others so much better at the language and more natural at picking up its subtleties. I stuck with the class through my four years in high school, even when budget cuts began to cut back on the availability later in my junior year.

Standing out was not my goal—in fact, flying under the radar sounded like a good plan to me. My French teacher would have none of that though, as I was one of the few males to make it through to the senior year. This year the teacher decided we would learn the French play *The Barber of Seville* and I would play the lead, Le Count Almaviva. In and of itself, my anxieties would make this a difficult proposition.

After much discussion and convincing from the teacher, I agreed to take on the part. She was convinced I could do it and had the utmost faith in me. My overdeveloped sense of not wanting to let my teacher down kicked in, and I plunged ahead.

I quickly learned that I was given the biggest part in the play by far. I had almost two-thirds of the lines! We would perform the play for several evening performances with full period costumes and sets, and if that wasn't enough, later we learned we would also perform several performances during the day for our fellow students! No pressure. No anxiety.

I was terrified at first but found an inner strength that allowed me to press on. I figured out that no one was going to know what I was saying anyway, so there was not going to be much pushback—at least I hoped.

This experience truly forged an ability to block out my surroundings and focus on the task at hand. I performed the play several times to the triumphant cheers of fellow students and night show crowds . . . until one of the final performances when I drew a blank in the middle of the play and needed help with my line from our teacher offstage.

She whispered the line several times, and I kept the deer-in-the-headlights look, attempting to hear what she said, until I blurted out "What?" Mind you, we are performing completely in French . . . and I blurted out in English! After the comic relief from the scene, even I was laughing at that mistake. That showing ended with a successful round of applause.

No matter what issues you may have, all can be overcome when you employ proper preparation and believe in yourself. Perhaps you will be lucky enough to do a play completely in French, and no one will know if you make a mistake—unless you pop in some English and destroy the mood of the play!

Emotional Times

My high school years were filled with mixed emotions that ran from the darkest to the brightest of life. I had built some tall emotional walls to hide behind over the years, and during high school, they began to show the wear of the emotional pressure I hid from the world. Looking back on things, I see my anxieties and fears needlessly clouded my judgment and trust of others.

I traversed the school year avoiding the situations most people gravitated toward. My schoolmates commonly socialized at school dances and impromptu gatherings. An unexplained phobia caused me to avoid these situations, though I did attend smaller youth group gatherings at church. I was truly fearful of what others would think of me and my choices.

What if I liked one person, and they didn't like me? What if everyone made fun of me for liking someone? I had seen people put into categories when they made poor choices. I didn't want to be labeled. Low self-esteem and anxiety continued to grow larger than anything I'd felt before. With this outlook, I found everything I was seeking—all the reasons I was not worthy of friendship, relationships, even existing on earth.

One of the memories that built this emotional house of cards came from targeting. A few years prior, I was contacted about coming to a social gathering at an upperclassman's house. I didn't know this person other than I assumed she was popular, being a cheerleader. I didn't go to the event and received a call from her. What I learned during the subsequent conversation was that I was chosen along with the others due to my shy, introverted nature. She had set up this experiment for a sociology class assignment and she wanted to know why I didn't want to attend. I was the only one who did not show up.

Knowing I was targeted as an introvert and an interesting experimental "lab rat" to be studied caved my self-esteem. I built a new level to increase the protective layer of my emotional wall. This conversation stayed with me and eroded my trust in others for some time. All I could think about was how lucky I had been to "dodge a bullet" and not be a victim of the "cool kids" making a mockery out of me. I wasn't going to play in their game. How could a teacher approve a project like this? My towering fortress would not let others see inside easily.

In my junior year, our church youth group went on a yearly ski trip. I was riding with a friend, Tracy, with whom I had a complex relationship. She was the first person I ever danced with at a youth group social, and I had mixed feelings toward her as possible girlfriend material, but she also came close to a "sister I never had." I felt comfortable talking to her on many levels.

This trip took a dark turn as the subject came up of possible crushes. I did all I could to avoid the subject and not show any emotion regarding crushes I might have had. Somehow the subject of my neighbor came up, and my face became cherry red. This betrayal of my emotions embarrassed me even more. The teasing began, and I felt pain unlike any I'd experienced before. It wasn't so much the subject matter of my neighbor—she was quite beautiful and a catch for anyone lucky enough to win her over. My pain came from not being able to hide behind the walls I had constructed for my protection, a pain of betrayal, not of teasing.

We broke up the trip home with a dinner break, and Tracy and I were separated into different cars for the rest of the trip. When the story came up about my emotional outburst due to the teasing, I appreciated the care and concern of others. But I kept the true reason for the pain well hidden behind the walls only I could know.

The rest of the year, I avoided most situations and interactions with Tracy and acted like I was not bothered by the distance. This choice, designed to "protect" myself, only served to alienate an important person in my life, the only one who kept trying to knock down my emotional walls. I didn't know how to repair my emotional immaturity.

My senior year a situation proved the ultimate summation of all things high school to me when, out of nowhere, a fellow senior turned to me in a history class and paid me a compliment while confirming my wallflower efforts. Kathy, a well-respected multi-sport player, turned to me one day and said, "You know, I didn't realize you were as funny as you are. I would have voted for you as the shyest guy in the class during the mock elections, but I didn't really know you." It made me laugh, as it revealed the efficacy of my protective shell.

THE WORST DAY EVER

The summer between my junior and senior year I experienced my "come to Jesus" moment. By far this was the lowest point in my life, and the culmination of all the walls I had built and protection I had intended. Instead, it was the day my walls were destroyed, and the light came back in full focus.

For weeks, my thoughts had begun to disturb me as I could not shake an abject fear I had of what others would think of my decisions. Darkness and fear began to consume me, and as I tried to find a way out, I continued to spiral more out of control with little hope of rescue.

A pity-party, self-loathing, no-way-out-of-the-situation feeling was all I could understand and see for the longest time. I had too much time on my hands and little else to do but think about my future or lack of a vision about it. I remember specifically sitting in the upstairs bathroom of our house one day and imagining what life would be like without me in the picture. Tears began to flow as I did not see a future. The deepest darkest pain I had ever felt consumed my thoughts and heart. There was no way anyone would want me as a boyfriend or future partner. There is no way *anyone* would want *me*!

I continued to cry as I explored ways to end my life as neatly as possible. I even had a razor to my wrist and envisioned myself in the bathtub passing peacefully and quickly so no one would have to worry about me again. Truly the lowest point in my life. Was this when it was all going to end?

I was at the proverbial bottom of the pit, and only one person could save me from this. A calm, powerful voice came to me. Not an audible voice you hear when speaking directly with another person, but an internal voice I can only describe as a heavenly life vest being sent to me in my time of need.

The voice was clear, "Mike . . . Don't do this. . . I have a greater plan for you." I looked around but didn't see anyone. My tears began to dissipate, and a wave of peace and calm came over me I can only describe as otherworldly. Then I heard it again, "Mike . . . Don't do this . . . I have a greater plan for you."

The voice was reassuring and calming and all-powerful. The pain and darkness began to break up and flake away. I put the razor away and pulled myself together. I wiped the tears from my face and splashed water on my cheeks to clean this pain from my body. From this point, I decided to begin to look on the brighter side of life.

I never spoke about this situation to anyone for the shame in what I was thinking about doing. I began to think of who might have found me if I had gone through with the act. All I could think was how unfair it would be to that person who found me and the trauma it would have brought to them. My family did not deserve to find me dead at my own hand, and I didn't want to put my pain onto them for the rest of their lives. This is another strong example of how thinking of others and doing for others gives more powerful energy to truly live by.

I knew there was a greater plan for me directly from God himself. . . . But what is that plan and how can he possibly take this mess that is me and do something with it? Now is the time to engage my faith, and trust was my first thought. I decided to find at least one thing each day I could be thankful for or find the positive side of life that only can be appreciated by someone who cherishes and looks forward to the future. This was going to be a difficult task, especially at first, and finding something each day to be thankful for proved difficult.

As I sought the positive, my life began to fill with more positivity, and I found it easier to find the positive in life. If you are experiencing something difficult in life—a loss, a change in status, betrayal, or any negative energy directed at your life—I advise you to give this a try and begin to find just one positive thing you can use as a rock to hold on to during the storms of life. You may not feel immediate relief, but trust me, you will come out the other end of the trial with a better understanding that there is a higher power in control and see how God can protect you from these trials and bring you safely through the storms.

If you feel these kinds of feelings, please talk to someone. If you don't have anyone close you feel you can talk to, several national phone banks are willing to listen to you and help you work out your depression. One thing I learned the hard way: everyone has a purpose in life and there is a plan for every life. You may not become a household name, but you may be the difference in one person's life, and honestly, that is an awesome feeling you don't want to miss.

− 8 −
College Recruitment

— 8 —
College Recruitment

I went into my senior year excited, knowing it was going to be my last in high school and hoping it was not my last one in football as a kicker. Realistically, very few get to move on after high school to play college football, and even fewer still move on to a professional career. I wanted to break through that ceiling and prove I was worthy.

As the season progressed, I began to get some letters from colleges. Schools I had never heard of before said they wanted me to consider coming to their school and playing football on their team. I kept waiting for all the Division I schools to call, but I received invitations mostly from NCAA Division III schools—a nice feeling all the same. It was just a matter of time before the Division I schools would start recruiting me; I was sure of it.

Then one day it happened. I received a letter from the University of Kentucky that they wanted me to come to Kentucky and kick for them! I was over the moon! It was not an official offer, but the preliminary feeling-out letter. I was sure the formal offer was just around the corner.

My coach said he had heard from them and was going to get some film together to send off and see what would happen. I asked him for his opinion on my chances. He told me he thought I'd make a "good Division III kicker."

What? A "good" Division III kicker? Are you kidding? I thought to myself, I am Division I material, and I'm going to prove it to you! From that point on, I worked harder in practice and took everything seriously so I could prove to the coach and the world, I was a top-caliber NCAA Division I kicker!

I continued to receive a couple of letters from Kentucky and believed they were going to offer me a scholarship to play DI football soon. My plan for my life was coming together perfectly! The offer never materialized. Worse yet, there was a coaching change at Kentucky and communications went silent.

The new coach was a former coach at the University of Maryland, Jerry Claiborne. I took this circumstance as a sign from God that this was to be. I grew up a few miles away from the University of Maryland and visited the Maryland Dairy and got ice cream cones as a child with my parents. It had to be the closure of the circle of life and a reuniting of Maryland superstars.

Some time passed, and I got the nerve to contact the new staff and see what was going on with the previous communication. I was met with a cordial greeting and then a bit of reality: "Coach Claiborne doesn't give scholarships to freshman kickers. You are more than welcome to walk on and compete for a scholarship, but there are no guarantees."

Well, how do you like that? Didn't they know I was originally from Maryland? This was meant to be a collaboration and successful teaming! I didn't like it one bit, to be honest with you, but it made me rethink my path yet again and realize perhaps *my* plan wasn't the plan I was destined for.

I continued to receive recruitment letters from several other colleges as well as a continued push from Adrian College, which happened to be about an hour and a half from our home. I even received what is probably the most gracious rejection letter from THE University in Alabama my Uncle Jimmy had tried to get to recruit me. The letter was a handwritten note from none other than Coach Paul "Bear" Bryant himself stating how their roster was already full with four kickers, and the NCAA has a limited number of scholarships they allow schools to have. I felt like it was almost an apology letter for not being able to extend a recruiting arm to me, though I understood the restrictions. It was one of the most treasured rejection letters I have ever received, and it taught me a lesson about how to treat people when you have negative news. **A little kindness and a full explanation of the situation will go a long way in giving a person some negative news while still lifting them with dignity.**

The letters from Adrian College came most frequently and were signed by Coach Heckert. Adrian was a small Division III school of about 1100 students at the time in southeastern Michigan. This was before the advent of the internet and email, so I hadn't heard much about the school or the football program until I visited the campus.

I remember the campus was small, about two city blocks including the dorms and scholastic buildings. They didn't have a football stadium on campus; they shared a community field with the local high school. It was a good field, don't get me wrong, and probably one of the best in the league I later found out.

My first visit was led by a student tour guide and soon-to-be graduate of the school and member of the football team, Mike Duffy. He later became a graduate assistant coach and eventually the athletic director at the school. I liked that I could remember his name, Mike, easy enough, and he gave my dad and me much insight into the school and the football program.

During the visit, I learned Coach Heckert had left the team to take a position with the Cleveland Browns and Coach K would be meeting with me. I was a little confused that I hadn't heard about this transition until now, but our talk was good, and I felt like this was a good place for me to be. The football team seemed to be on its way up with an undefeated season two years ago and only one loss the previous season. It sounded like their program was growing and would be an honor to be a part of.

I left campus with a good feeling about the school and the program but questioned who was going to be leading the program next, and whether I would like him? As time went on, a third coach came into the picture who became the new head coach, Coach Labadie. I had no connection to him and no recruiting communication from him before making my decision. Blind faith is an amazing thing, but I knew I wanted Adrian to be my home and wanted to feel peace in my soul about the decision. I wasn't sure how this was part of God's plan, but I trusted it would be the right decision—I was about 80 percent convinced anyway.

A Push towards Adrian

In my senior year, another church youth group ski weekend was scheduled, and most of the students going were underclassmen. Tracy was the one person who gave me mixed feelings about going. After my bout of deep depressive thoughts, I determined I needed to bury the hatchet with her and get over any negative feelings. I had missed my friend during the school year since the strained ski weekend.

I was still new to this outward expression, but I hoped God would give me the strength and words to say to her. We were going to Irish Hills near Adrian for cross country and downhill skiing. Still rather awkward around her, I managed to clear the air between us and apologize for my cold nature for the last few months. I was not sure if things would ever be the same, but I wanted to clear the slate and begin to follow God's plan to open myself to others. She was always trying to get me out of my shell, but my walls were too thick, and I was too immature to let her in.

An interesting situation happened that weekend that forever changed my life. Marsha, a freshman and a friend of Tracy's sister, went with the group to downhill ski. Marsha came back to the cabins with a sore leg after a fall on the slopes. She hobbled back to her room where she rested before mealtime. What happened next is a little fuzzy to me, but I was in my room resting after a morning of cross-country skiing around the grounds. Tracy asked if I could assist Marsha in getting up to the dining hall.

I went over to her room to see what had happened. I entered the room and listened to Marsha tell the story of her fall for what must have been the umpteenth time. As a fellow athlete, I asked if she needed some ice and made sure she elevated her leg to protect it. She was cordial and thanked me for the advice.

Another group of people came barging through the door to see the spectacle that was now the ski slope accident. The room was abuzz, and the commotion and attention were beginning to get to Marsha. She had her fill and snapped and told everyone to get out of her room.

Her friend, Toni, joined in and ensured full compliance, seeing everyone out. Then Marsha spoke up and said, "Mike, you don't have to leave if you don't want to." Honestly, I was surprised about being singled out. Since I didn't have any place to go, I stayed and kept trying to figure out how I could be helpful. This was something different and a new and unfamiliar position to me.

I tried to talk to her to keep her mind off the injury and offered to help her around as a crutch when she needed it. She agreed, and

I felt useful on a new level. During the day we went to the dining hall a couple of times, and she leaned on me as a crutch to get her from place to place. I was able to talk to her like I had never talked with a girl before, and we laughed and joked about many subjects and discussed sports and dreams. I had never connected with someone so quickly in my life.

Even through all her pain, Marsha kept a cheerful and upbeat attitude that was truly inspiring for someone in her condition. The thing I most remember about her was her electric smile that could light up any room she was in. Her leg did not improve through the day. After dinner, the chaperones on the trip decided they needed to take her to the hospital to get it checked out.

Toni came to my room and asked if I'd help her down to the car. I jumped at the chance and felt a lump in my throat that she had to get checked out at the hospital. I remember feeling like I wanted to go to the hospital with her, like a protective older brother or something, to be of comfort in some way. That wasn't in the plans.

When I delivered her to the car, I wished her well and headed back to the room. I remember feeling a longing for her and hoped for the best but knew it was something serious. At that point, I stood at my bunk and looked out the window and began to pray God would help heal her knee and give the doctors the care and patience to take good care of her. I also felt a wave come over me at that point that this is where I need to go to college. Adrian College was where God wanted me to go as part of HIS plan.

I thought, Why not? My family attended a United Methodist church at the time, and Adrian was affiliated with the United Methodist Council. It was also going to be close enough for my family and friends to come to see me play and enjoy the journey with me. These serendipities provided confirmation to reassure my soul.

Marsha returned to the cabin sometime after midnight after we had gone to sleep. The next morning there was a knock at the door, and Toni asked if I could help Marsha up to the dining hall as Marsha didn't want to use her crutches in the snow. I again jumped at the chance and came over and helped her around camp the rest of the day before going home.

It was a weekend that didn't have much skiing on my part, but I was good with not skiing. I was able to get to know a person who I will forever hold in high esteem for her positive nature and electric smile that truly spread joy everywhere she went. I wanted to fill my life with this kind of spirit and joy and felt like a new person with a new outlook on life after that weekend.

I realized that caring for other people and worrying less about what others think of me was the greatest gift I could get out of this encounter. The events of that weekend proved a turning point in my life. It cemented my acceptance of God's plan for my life and set me on a path to the positive attitude that would serve me well throughout the rest of my life.

— 9 —
The Adrian Experience

— 9 —
The Adrian Experience

I had learned on the ski trip how to ensure my college experience started on a good note, not like high school. I had opened up to others more and looked for the positives so they would come more frequently. My first experience on campus was at freshman orientation weekend. There were several groups to choose from, manageable and diverse enough for students to get to know each other and start to form bonds they could enjoy during the next four years. The weekend was a microcosm of the college experience. We ate in the dining hall, slept in the dorms, had lectures in the classrooms, and were treated to after-hours social programs.

Saturday night we had a mixer dance in the student union. As was typical of the time, boys and girls would traditionally stand separate, chatting and speculating on who would make the first move. There were some really cute girls there that weekend and a few truly elite lookers. All night I kept telling myself to be open and don't build any walls—this was college after all.

Then my darkest fear reared its ugly head—I was asked to dance. Mind you, I was ready to slow dance with anyone who asked, but this was a fast dance. To make it worse, I was asked by the prettiest girl there that weekend! God has a sense of humor I will never figure out, but I was going to be open to new experiences, so I accepted. Probably not the best choice for my self-esteem, as I was never a graceful dancer.

Dancing was not a gift I was given at birth, but I tried. She was super nice but kept telling me to loosen up and giving me critiques as we danced. Don't get me wrong, I appreciated being asked. God must have been prodding me to keep an open mind about things. I may not have expected the lesson, but God sure has a flair for delivering the message. The rest of the weekend was nondescript, but in the end, I knew this was where I was supposed to be, and I had high hopes the best was yet to come.

Football REALITY vs FANTASY

I arrived at camp a few days into the official start of summer camp. They told me I didn't need to report right away as they had a senior quite accomplished at the position, so I wasn't expected to play much my freshman year.

Head Coach Labadie, a no-nonsense type of person, had a history with the college as an accomplished former player and successful high school coach from Marshall, Michigan. He was even a member of the Adrian College Athletic Hall of Fame. I hoped this would translate to a path of success for our team.

Coach Lyall, my position coach throughout my career at Adrian, also coached the defensive line. He had a successful career at the University of Michigan coached by the legendary Bo Schembechler. Coach Lyall brought that same intensity and joy of the game to Adrian and helped infuse a winning attitude in all our players. Throughout the camp, Coach Lyall kept encouraging me and gave me one of my favorite quotes, "Kick through it, not to it." I had a habit of short-legging my kicks, which affected their trajectory.

Coach Lyall also coached strength and conditioning, running us through a routine he called "The Edge." This variety of conditioning routines got everyone in game shape quickly during camp as he incorporated it every third practice. It was as if he had gone back in time to consult a leader of the Spanish Inquisition to get the most heinous torture anyone could devise. Well, it wasn't that bad, but during our time in the trenches, it felt that way! This helped us become one of the best-conditioned teams in any game we played and it gave us trainees the "edge" in many ways that would prove a winning combination for us all.

I had a rough start to my career and always felt one step behind everyone after arriving late to camp. For reasons I could not answer, I started kicking and the ball would take a strange trajectory off my shoe without the normal rotations. I didn't have long to figure it out when Jon, the senior kicker, came down with a staph infection in his knee, so he was laid up in the hospital and out of commission during camp.

My self-confidence began to fail. No matter how hard I tried, I could not kick a decent kick for an extra point, field goal, or kickoff during this time. My kicks were spinning with a spiral or upright like a tornado, and nothing had a high trajectory. The harder I tried, the worse it seemed to get. The situation demoralized me and got me too into my head. On top of my trials, as a late-comer and new kid on campus and hadn't gotten to know many of the other players.

I was at a loss and not sure I was going to make it as a college football player. Frustrated and somewhat embarrassed by the end of the week, I asked Coach Labadie if I could take some footballs over the weekend to the practice field to try and figure out what was going on with my situation. He agreed and gave me a bagful.

I came to Adrian with high expectations for myself and wanted a chance to prove I deserved to be here. Too wrapped up in my faults and failures, I could not focus on the job at hand and make a consistent effort. I desperately wanted to create a successful aura around my abilities.

I went out on Sunday afternoon and tried to work things out on the practice field. No luck. Same results . . . spirals, tornados, and no-height kicks were all the norm. Frustrated, I began to talk to myself and God to ask what was going on. I was not playing to my ability. I had not shown up to play college football expecting to pan out as some kind of fake.

I walked around a little to clear my head, and then a thought came to me. What about trying it barefoot? Hummmmm. I'm not sure why the crazy idea came to me; I just knew something had to change with my kicking or I'd never make it on the team. I was told it was illegal in Michigan high school football to kick barefoot, but this is college football, and it is legal here! (I hoped!)

I looked around to see if anyone was around watching. No one that I could see. I'll try it once and see how it goes, I bargained with myself. There has to be something special about this. I hope it doesn't hurt my foot, I thought. I quickly pulled off my right cleat and then my sock. I remember a warm feeling on my foot that felt like a summer day back in Maryland in my old backyard.

Just keep your head down and follow through. Kick through it, not to it. Piece of cake.

I stared at the ball and visualized the perfect kick. I approached, swung my leg, and made contact on the top of my foot perfectly. My leg stretched out in perfect follow-through, just like I visualized. My head was down, but I knew there was something different about this kick. As I looked up to see the ball flying through the air, I noticed a perfect slow-rotation, end-over-end high kick making its way to the end zone. It looked like a 55- to

60-yard kick, but there were no markings on the practice field at the time, so that was just an estimate. From that point on, I knew this was my new kicking style! And the best part was, it didn't hurt my foot! I made several more kicks, all with the positive results I knew I had in me. I couldn't wait to unveil it at practice on Monday!

At practice, I sprung this new kicking style on Coach Lyall in the pre-practice warm-ups. He had a look about him at first, and then shook his head and said, "If you want to try it, go for it."

I had heard about some barefoot kickers at that time, Tony Franklin being the most famous, but not many in the state of Michigan. "What are you going to do when it gets cold out?" was one comment. I'll deal with that when the time comes.

For now, this helped me concentrate more and that helped my performance, so my confidence began to grow. Though my time on the first team was short-lived, it was the perfect push I needed to start the journey I was destined to follow. Jon, the senior kicker, returned with a healed knee, back to booming the ball each time. I was showing myself as a better kicker with my new style, but he had the experience.

Jon, a great mentor for me during the year, taught me many subtle nuances of being a college kicker like the art of stretching, looking busy, and most importantly, having a strong resolve and confidence in yourself as the one the team will count on during crunch time. Jon went on to become the First Team Michigan Intercollegiate Athletic Association (MIAA) All-League kicker that year.

Years later I understood having Jon ahead of me started off my college career on great footing. If I were to have tried to kick anywhere else, they would have dismissed me on my initial kicking. I probably wouldn't have been given much of a chance after my shabby initial results and learning curve. Instead, I had a whole year to perfect and grow into my kicking style and become a more confident kicker. Besides, I was sure I'd have a chance to play and get some experience sometime that first year.

Game day was quite a spectacle as our whole team dressed for home games. The majority of us were relegated to cheering for the players ahead of us unless injuries or a blowout were happening. Then the coaches would give some playing time to the lower string players. My barefoot kicking was getting noticed, and I was on the depth chart as the second-string kicker. All year I waited for my opportunity. I was not asked to join the travel squad at away games, as they took the third-string kicker who was also the second-string punter and third-string quarterback . . . more potential help if needed. I sort of understood it but still wanted to get in and play.

I ended the year playing in the JV games and making all three of my extra points with no field goal attempts. At the end of the year, I had the distinction of being the only person on the team who did not play a single play on the varsity team that year. Out of 110 guys—like ten percent of the campus—I was the *only* one not to play a single play on varsity. **God had a message for me about patience in there somewhere.**

When the reality of the season set in, I got a little frustrated, a little ashamed, and a little sad I did not get a chance to do something for the team. I began to question my loyalty to the program and whether I should explore new venues for my talent. Someone had to have a need for a kicker. Someone would appreciate me and my talents. Perhaps I should have walked on at Kentucky after all. I wondered if it were too late.

But then I thought, if I work hard, I can show everyone what they missed last year and be the best kicker Adrian has ever had. A rush of emotion and a tingle in my spine came over me (the first of many), and I knew in my heart that Adrian was the place I was destined to be to make a significant impact.

I attacked the off-season with a renewed sense of purpose and striving to be the best I could be. That summer, I ran more during off-season training than I ever had. I took winding paths around my hometown of Fenton, and my route took me past the community center and tennis courts. Many times, teens and twenty-somethings were hanging out smoking—a rather intimidating group.

Several times I was a target of their jeers. "Why are you running?" "You are not very fast!" "You might as well quit—you'll never be anything!" (That one hit a nerve and hurt/motivated me the most.)

As I fielded the quips running on their perimeter, *I'll show you,* kept running through my head. I steeled myself, *I'm going to make something of myself. What are you going to do with your life?*

Many times, I used this as fuel for my mental workouts, making sure I had the fire burning hot to improve and make a difference in the coming football campaign. I'd finish the workouts with a tingle in my spine, knowing I had done my best and something good would result.

I learned that one's mental strength needed to be as strong as the physical, if not more. I always said kicking is 50 percent physical and 80 percent mental . . . before you check the math, I'm a kicker and am smart enough to know that is more than 100 percent. **The true lesson was learning that mental strength is the difference between becoming a good or great kicker.**

FRESHMAN DORM LIFE

My playing time was not what I expected or wanted my freshman year, but football was not the only reason I attended Adrian. I lived in one of the dorms known as the Freshman Quad in Davis Hall. This was a three-floor coed dorm with a good mixture of people from several surrounding states, students with diverse backgrounds and an equal range of goals and studies.

The dorm had several common areas including the front lobby with couches and tables for studying, socializing, and playing euchre card games that lasted well into the night. We also had a television room that was mostly fixed on MTV—back when the channel actually played music videos and had the original music VJs delivering the hits and backstories on the artists of the day. Many students could be found lounging on the sectional couches between classes and meals watching music videos.

My dorm mates and I experienced this new life in a socially interactive hive of activity. We enjoyed the spontaneity of the social interactions and freely circulated from room to room getting to know our fellow Bulldogs. We forged friendships that would grow stronger over the years, even after graduation. Some would not graduate with us, but still, the common experience forged a special friendship that would continue long afterwards. Going to the dining hall for our three meals a day was a great way to get to know our new family around cafeteria food. But when that didn't hit all cylinders, many times we would also run out for a late-night pizza run or other fast-food snack.

We learned to navigate the idiosyncrasies of fellow students. We had our share of extroverts who tried to get everyone involved in most of the activities and who sought to include the wallflowers and in-betweeners who were learning how to navigate the new social environment. I made a conscious effort to step out of my comfort zone and try to be part of the dorm life.

Gina, one of the most outgoing people I have ever met in my life, coached me in this new endeavor. This marketing major was a natural at promoting an inclusive environment. Gina and I had several classes together freshman year and ended up in many more classes throughout our college career. She introduced me to other Davis Hall residents and made my transition to a functioning member of the dorm easier. Her assistance took the edge off of my new resolution to be more social.

CW, another person I met that year, resided on the other end of the social spectrum. Intellectually, CW was probably one of the smartest people in our class and, next to Robbie from New Carrollton, one of the most intelligent people I have ever known. I'm not sure the exact reason our friendship grew, but we seemed to be kindred spirits. The best part was watching CW's social evolution over the years as he became one of the most socially outgoing people by the end of our college career.

I passed Bill in the hallways and knew him from a distance through the year. What drew us together at the end of the year housing selections for our sophomore year—neither of us had a roommate. Both of our freshman roommates chose to do something different, so we were suggested to room together. We proved a perfect fit for roommates for the rest of our college experience. This friendship became a brother-from-another-mother relationship that would last for life.

We found plenty of opportunities to get to know dormmates from watching MTV in the basement community TV lounge to euchre card tournaments in the main floor lounge/study area. We bounced from room to room socializing, talking about classes, and getting to know each other. There was even a group of us who had a mud football game in the quad outside our dorm after a rainstorm, and we ended up hanging out in the TV room all night before going to the dining hall for breakfast the next morning. Not the best presentation as we mingled with some outside attendees of a conference in the cafeteria line prior to their meeting. The outsiders must have chuckled at our appearance and tired looks as we meandered through the breakfast line while they chatted us up as we walked together. This common experience was one of the memories that solidified my belief that Adrian was the place I was supposed to be, and I made the right decision for my college experience.

— 10 —
Running Into a Challenge

— 10 —
Running Into a Challenge

August and summer camp had arrived. As a sophomore, I was the most senior kicker on the roster, aiming to make my mark and reveal the results of my intense summer workouts. The coaches and teammates would see my improvements and my abilities. I was about to take my place on the starting team, an easy slam dunk from here. This was some of the hype I heard in my head until I arrived for summer camp workouts.

I arrived to quite a surprise and shock when I learned of a freshman kicker on campus. Not just any kicker, but a guy named Frank from California who was All-Northern California—the equivalent of an all-state kicker from Michigan. That threw up a hurdle that stood a little higher than I expected.

I didn't have the credentials or the awards he had, and I assumed he must be better than me in talent. At least those were the thoughts running through my head at first. Why would God bring me through the best summer training I had ever had only to let me fall on my face in front of everyone and continue to be the only guy who didn't play a single time on the varsity team?!

Something inside me answered that question quickly: God didn't do that to me, and I have the power to do all things through God who strengthens me! Besides that, God has a greater plan—for me! My insecure self began to sit down a little and the stronger me stood up.

This wasn't going to be easy, but nothing is when you have a purpose. I was doing this for my family, friends, and all the shy introverts of the world. I wanted them to look outside themselves and learn they have the power to do great. It can and will happen!

As destiny would have it, my consistency through camp with the new barefoot kicking style gave me an edge. I fought hard and had doubts at times only to have a higher power pull me along and let me know I wasn't alone in this journey—an amazing feeling when you understand and believe in the plan God has for you.

It was finally the first week of the season, when the coaches would decide who would start. It came down to a few days before the game, and the coach gave me the nod. My first hurdle crossed! God brought me through this. I was so thankful and humbled and knew the best was yet to come. I was cool on the outside, but an internal party raged in my soul!

Starter Status

I played my first game as a starter versus Otterbein, a small college in Ohio just outside of Columbus. I remember meeting the start of the day with anticipation and excitement, about to realize my dream of playing college football. I was grateful for the opportunity—an opportunity to display my skills and to give my friends and relatives something to point to and say I knew him when . . . proud in knowing they were a part of what I was about to show the world.

I would go into battle with a strong core around me I felt comfortable with. There was senior Jeff Hood as my holder and fellow sophomore Steve Bohl as the long snapper. I was the new cog in this machine since Jon Petticrew graduated, earning the First-Team All-MIAA Placekicker the previous year. He had set a high precedent for me, and I wanted to do my best to continue the success the kicking team had achieved the last year.

I specifically remember our free time before the pregame warm-ups, just after arriving at the facility and receiving our time-line for pregame activities. I walked into the hallway of the gym-nasium—alone—with pride and anticipation of what could be the realization of my dreams. I came across a trophy case display of the college denoting team and individual awards. I remem-ber specifically seeing a plaque with the name and positions of the All-American awards, past student-athletes from the school. One was a kicker—a Kodak All-American Kicker. I don't recall his name; I just know the feeling I felt to see his status as an All-American.

SETTING A GOAL

I stared at this plaque for several minutes then began to feel something I had never felt before. My spine began to tingle, and my eyes began to well up with tears. Achieving an All-American status as a kicker is what I wanted to give my family, friends back in Maryland and Fenton, and new friends at Adrian, the desire to my core. I wanted them to be able to say they know an All-Amer-ican football player and feel the pride the same as I would by achieving this goal.

How was I going to do that? We had an All-American player on our team the previous year, defensive lineman Jim Nowaske—a mountain of a man. I was so glad I was on his team and not play-ing against him. I didn't know any other All-American football players myself, and who was I to assume a shy, introverted person like myself would be able to achieve a noble goal like this?

I was not a hulking player myself. The only person I could

think of was the ultimate power . . . the One who created everything and has the power to achieve anything. I stood there and had a conversation with God and humbly asked if it is His will that I would be able to do this as a gift to my family, those still here and those already gone from this world, and my friends growing up who meant the world to me and new people who had come into my life never knowing me as an introvert. This conversation infused in me something I can only describe as supernatural grace. My spine tingled as a feeling of peace came over me that I still cannot explain, and tears of joy began to trickle down my face.

I knew half the battle was won. The rest was for me to put faith into action and focus on the task at hand. How it would end up, I had no clue, but I did know I was in good hands.

The pregame warm-ups were focused and deliberate. I was ready to do my part when called on, and called on I was. The offense moved the ball well but struggled to get it in the end zone that day. I ended up kicking four field goals, making three of them from 34, 39, and 32 yards. The other was blocked when a blocker lined up across from the wrong person, allowing a defender to get through. This glaring example illustrated how it takes eleven people working together and doing their assigned positions to make this unit work. I learned quickly, this journey wasn't about me—I was just one person out of eleven that will make this unit successful.

It became my nature to remain humble and thankful for anything I could achieve. The game was hard fought, with the defense holding Otterbein College to seven points. We won the game nine to seven!

Post-Game Celebration

It seemed like most everyone on the team slapped me on the helmet or back congratulating me on the three field goals by the end of the game, and the cheers overwhelmed me that day knowing I was part of this win and did my job in helping the team. Quite a feeling comparing my first college game to last year's season watching from the sidelines each week. This was only the beginning of quite an emotional night!

As I was jogging off the field, someone from the media sought me out to ask my reactions to the game. I was floored. Internally, I was screaming, but I managed to hold my outer demeanor steady. I had heard as a kicker you cannot let your emotions get too high or too low—you need to live on an even keel. I spoke to the reporter but had no recollection of what I said moments after completing the interview.

Later I was told I sounded like a seasoned veteran . . . just another day at the office. Honestly, it was all a blur. I knew my grandpa saw this from heaven and my parents from the stands, and I wanted to share this feeling with them. I finally found them in the sea of people on the field, the traditional meeting place for friends and families at Division III football games. My parents were proud of me and all I was able to do with the team that day.

We exchanged pleasantries, and they gushed over my performance as any proud parent would do. Next, they told me how Marsha, the girl from the ski weekend and reason behind choosing Adrian College, was in the hospital with what they thought could be spinal meningitis. I had no idea what this was, but it didn't sound good at all. This was the person who truly changed my life by accepting me for who I was. She had allowed me to help her, and it opened my eyes from there forward. Life was

80

not about feeling sorry for myself but about helping and lifting others.

I rode the bus ride back to Adrian among quite a rowdy and festive crew after our win. However, I sat alone, subdued, and looking out the window for the majority of the time, reflecting on the day's events, thanking God for giving me the ability to do what I did, but most of all, asking him to please help Marsha with whatever was affecting her and to make her well. Again, I realized it wasn't about me; it was about helping others.

VALIDATION

We arrived back at the dorm, and what awaited me was truly emotional as well. My friends in the dorm and around campus had taken paper towels from the restroom and fashioned a banner across my dorm door filled with congratulatory messages and pride in knowing me! This banner was truly an inspiration and lift to my heart that night and verified why I wanted to be the best I could be—to lift my family and friends through my actions. I knew I had a new home and began to feel like I was a part of something special.

I experienced many highs after that game. I was awarded the Bulldog Special Teams Player of the Week and found a new, unfamiliar popularity around campus. It seemed everyone knew who I was, and many took the opportunity to congratulate me on my performance in that game. It continued through the season. Honestly, most of the people congratulating me I did not know personally, but I did the gentlemanly thing I was taught, smiling and saying "thank you" for the well wishes.

I truly did appreciate the recognition but knew I had to stay humble and not let this recognition go to my head. Fame honestly made me feel uneasy as I began to wonder if I would use it for my best interest or personal gain. My concerns caused me to put up a protective emotional wall as I had done before, though this time I knew I needed to keep an open mind and always look for the positive side of things.

I also had to guard against the negative spiral of walling myself off emotionally. At the same time, I had to trust God and my friends would protect me from the potential downfalls of fame. I had learned from my past mistakes and realized now I had a new set of friends that truly cared about each other. This was the support I was going to need and appreciate at Adrian and beyond.

The rest of the season was filled with more joy and activity for me as we progressed through the challenges and opponents. In week two, we took on Wooster College for our first home game of the season. Spirits were high going in off of a good week of preparation. We ended the game 34 to 7 in a game that our defense dominated and the offense rolled at will. My foot connected on two field goals that week. I had contributed, and I was beginning to feel more a part of the team than I ever had. I could sense I was living God's plan for my life.

Two Firsts

In the third game, we were going to play our toughest opponent to date in Westminster, an NCAA Division III powerhouse. I was able to connect on a field goal with eight minutes remaining to put us up 10–6. On the ensuing kickoff, I made my first tackle on a kickoff. The kick returner broke through the line, and, for some inexplicable reason, headed straight for me! Luckily, Jeff Hood, the holder and starting defensive back, stood behind me in case anyone got through our kick defense.

The sight of this kick returner running straight at me froze me in my tracks, and I tried to anticipate which way he might try to run around me. I stood solid, and he kept coming directly at me.

Why is he not trying to angle away from me? I thought. I braced myself for the inevitable. We made contact, and I wrapped my arms around for dear life. I hope he doesn't step on my bare foot and keeps going through my mind as well. I felt my body turn and move in the opposite direction toward the end zone as he dragged me a couple of yards but then collapsed under my meager added weight. I had made my first official tackle. The crowd and our sideline erupted when they noticed a barefoot kicker had made the tackle.

There was an emotional swing in our favor. Unfortunately, the Westminster offense collected themselves, drove down the field, and scored a touchdown to go up 13–10. It was up to our offense to take us down and win the game. The offense marched down the field in what appeared to be a game-winning drive. It would at least give me an opportunity to kick a tying field goal to take our chances in overtime. Unfortunately, we came up short at the 4-yard line when the game ended.

This was our first loss of the season. How would we react to this disappointment? I wanted to do my part and kick a field goal, but our offense didn't get us in position for a chance to tie the game. I continued to learn patience and understanding and to be ready at all times, even when I am not called on in a game-winning situation.

Our next game was another non-conference home game against St. Norbert from Wisconsin. One of the most complete games we played as a team all year resulted in a blowout 52–14

83

score. This was the only game I would play without my family in attendance. My parents attended the wedding of the oldest of our New Carrollton friends/family, Karen and husband Steve. I wanted to have gone, but knew it was important for my parents to attend and support the newlyweds, the first of the neighborhood kids to get married.

As it was, this was the perfect game for them to miss since we scored so much that my playing did not have a major role in the outcome. The most I got out of this game was a tired leg kicking so many extra points and kickoffs. This was a good primer and just what our team needed after last week's close loss. The next week would begin our MIAA championship quest.

— 11 —
Conference Competition

— 11 —
Conference Competition

Alma College was our first opponent, and they came in having a rough non-league result with one win and three losses. Their fighting attitude kept the game close. Our defense did what they did all year and kept their offense down all day. I was called on to kick an extra point and field goal which proved the difference in our 10–7 victory. I was able to help the team again and looked forward to our next game, which was homecoming. My performance again earned me the Special Teams Player of the Week.

Albion arrived at homecoming with an impressive win streak and stood on top of the league standings with us—for now. Our defense made a statement with their inspired clutch play. I had an opportunity to add a field goal but missed the mark.

I remember expressing frustration with the miss moments after the kick only to be brought back to reality by Jeff, my holder, with a forceful admonishment: "Don't worry about that kick. We may need your foot later, so keep your head in the game for the next one." My mind went in multiple directions, and my career flashed before my eyes as far back as the missed extra point from my last high school contest. I was determined not to make the same mistake, not with this team anyway.

I got my head screwed back on and worked on preparing for my next kick the rest of the game. Later we scored a single touchdown, and I was able to add an extra point for the margin to win versus a single field goal. This game taught me many points that day. One, I need to keep my emotions in check, especially during the game, because the team may need me to make a high-pressure kick at any time. Two, I belong to a team that stands with me, and we lift each other in all situations. Three, the past is the past—I cannot let any doubt creep into my psyche. That day reminded me to always keep positive thoughts.

Next on the schedule was Hope College. At the time, this was one of the rivalry games our team took to heart. Since Hope was a traditional powerhouse in our league, we knew that to be the best, you needed to beat the best. This was going to be a fight, and playing away put us at a disadvantage. But we had an air of confidence that we were the better team and just needed to play our game, and we did.

It was another difficult game with the defense leading the way, frustrating Hope's offense and shutting them out the first half. Our offense was able to move the ball, but not able to punch it in for touchdowns, so I was called on to kick field goals. I made two field goals of 22 and 19 yards to give us the advantage of 6–0 at halftime. The second half saw much the same effort on the part of our defense, which held Hope scoreless for the first time in their new home stadium and during their homecoming no less.

We were able to add a touchdown in the fourth quarter, but rather than kick an extra point, the coaches opted for a two-point conversion. The conversion failed and the final score ended 12–0, achieving an undefeated record in league play.

We enjoyed the euphoria all the way back to Adrian that night. I felt a sense of pride in helping the team again with two field goals and knew something special was brewing with this team and our goals for the season. I remember wishing I would have had a chance to add an extra point but understood the numbers game the coach had to strategize.

Our season record was progressing just as we wanted. How we got there was another story as we played some of the closest games many of us had experienced in our football careers. The next game was Olivet College, a bitter pill from the previous year when we lost on our home turf. This was a revenge game for us to make our mark on the season.

The league championship was within our grasp if we could win. We also might get it with some help if the second-place teams, Alma and Albion, lost once more. To close out another close game, our offense came up big throughout the day. We were able to move the ball well but stalled on three drives. I got the call with field goals of 25, 38, and 37 yards and two extra points during the game. Our team got up 29–27, and on the final drive of the game, Olivet threw a third interception that allowed us to run the clock out. We escaped with the win, but the closeness of the game gave us a nervous feeling.

I was ecstatic after the game knowing I gave it my all and helped the team with my kicks. I felt much as I had after the first game of the season and our close win. This game continued to add to my confidence level, and I knew God had been directing my path all season.

What we didn't know was both Alma and Albion had lost, thus giving us the league title before the final week of competition! As happy as we were with this news, we knew we still had to finish the season with a win to be perfect in league play. We prepared knowing it would be difficult to keep focus knowing we had already won the league championship.

We pulled ourselves together and played a solid game. Our offense moved the ball well and completed scores with touchdowns. I was able to contribute with three extra-point kicks. The score was closer than the game was expected to end as Kalamazoo scored on the last play of the game, but the final score closed at 21–18 in our favor.

What happened next was like a dream sequence from every championship movie with the congratulatory high fives, hugs, and celebratory pile-up of bodies crashing together in total joy and respect for achieving the ultimate league finale. The MIAA league trophy was presented to the team at midfield, and pictures galore were taken by media, family, and friends. The joyous celebration went on for some time.

The year was a magical one for me in that I ended the whole season at the top of the NCAA Division III statistics for kickers. I led the nation that year in field goals made per game. It was the first time anyone had led the nation in any category for football statistics in Adrian College's school history.

Part of the reason I was able to achieve this statistical feat was an offense that was able to move the ball up and down the field but had issues getting it into the endzone. The defense was a pillar for our team as well and statistically one of the best in the nation. Together we were able to win the Michigan Intercollegiate Athletic Association (MIAA) league that year for the sixth time in school history.

SURPRISE POST-SEASON PLAY

This year also saw Division III open the playoff slots to additional teams. For the first time in school history, we were chosen to be part of the national playoffs. We would be matched against the previous year's runner-up NCAA Division III National Champions, Augustana College. Flying to Rock Island, Illinois, for the game via Detroit through Chicago was a fantastic and surreal experience.

On game day, the local Rock Island paper had several articles previewing the game and one that particularly caught many eyes on our team. The article basically said Adrian had a "leg up" on Augustana. The article stated if it came down to a kick at the end of the game, we would have a leg up and opportunity to win due to my skills combined with the leg of our punter, Tom Wakeling. We had a one-two punch that gave our team an excellent chance to win any close game. Many on the team showed me the article, and they felt a higher level of confidence because they had seen what Tom and I were able to do throughout the season. My confidence level was raised a bit as well, and I looked forward to the game. Honestly, I had a few extra butterflies due to the article and secretly hoped it would not come down to a last-second kick, but I knew I had the ability and our team backing me if it did.

It was going to be the most competitive contest we would experience for the season, and the game's outcome did come down to the kicking game. The cool, damp weather made the field a bit on the messy side, but we both had to play on the same field, so that would not be an excuse for either team. The back-and-forth contest changed the lead with each score.

I made my three extra-point attempts that day. Augustana's kicker missed his first attempt, forcing them to go for a two-point conversion the next two times. Unfortunately for us, they succeeded on both attempts. By the end of the day, the score was 22–21. On the sidelines, we knew up to and after the closing buzzer that we had a chance to win the game. I had the belief of the team that if they could get the ball downfield close enough, I could make the kick to win the game. I was excited about the opportunity, but it never came.

In the end, we fell by one point. The magical season ended, but the rewards were about to flow. God has an excellent sense of humor and a nice way of congratulating a fine year. On our trip back, the team was split between two different planes. I was on a twin-engine prop plane with thirteen of my teammates. Kind of a scary operation when a puff of smoke blew out the back of the engines when they were started.

On this leg of the trip, though, we had a special passenger, the 1983 Miss USA titleholder. I was even lucky enough to have a seat in front of her on the plane. I will admit I had to "twist-stretch" in my seat and peek, in the hopes of every red-blooded American boy's fantasy—that if we started up a conversation, we would become fast friends. Of course, she was guarded by her handler on the aisle seat, but Miss USA slept all the way to Chicago. Now don't get me wrong, but with my history of shyness, I can honestly say I would not have had the time to get up the nerve to say anything suave and sophisticated to her. I just had to laugh that God squarely put me in the situation.

− 12 −
Rituals and Routines

— 12 —
Rituals and Routines

I was part of the special teams' group on the team known as the kickers and punters. Mind you, we kept up the competition and pushed to stay on our game throughout the year. We would practice often away from the team on mundane and repetitive aspects of kicking and punting, stretching, and mind games. I always say kicking is 50% physical and 80% mental. Yes, I know the math doesn't add up, but the mental aspect is key to success on the field. We would put ourselves through game simulations and scenarios to keep our skills sharp.

It looked easy to other players who were beating up on each other and trying to outduel each other in their position and team drills. I recognized this kicking repetition was going to be the key to keeping an even keel during heated situations. Kicking extra points for what seemed like forever gave me the discipline I would need later in my football and even work career to get the job done.

Kickers sometimes get a bad rap for being set in their ways and needing to do certain routines over and over. I'd like to say I was different, but that would not be totally accurate. You see, I enjoyed a few private and public routines that may leave some people scratching their heads or otherwise confused. All I can say is, they worked for me!

A kicking routine needs consistency and repetition. I carried this into my preparation for games and practiced some secretly and others not so much. Prior to the first game when I was named the starting kicker, after I showered and shaved my face, I looked down at my foot and noticed some hair on my foot. I thought, well if you shave your face to look better, why not your foot? It is going to be front and center in the game as well.

So, I took out the shaving cream and shaved my foot. Did it make a difference? I'm not sure. I just wanted to show some respect to the foot for the journey we were about to go on. And since you put cologne on after you shave, why not add some to your foot? So I did. Though we had a community bathroom on our dorm floor, no one was up or saw me do this, so my secret stayed safe.

After the results of the first game, though, I kept doing it as part of the routine because I didn't want to do anything different than I had done the previous week to mess with any mojo. During our first overnight away game, I had to share a room with my teammates. My foot-shaving routine was discovered and deemed a quirky thing only a kicker would do. After the first year, it became a must-do, and a tradition was born.

As for many athletes before practice and games, music was a major part of my pregame routine. I had a set of songs I listened to before every game, home and away. These songs had meaning and were an extension of me—a way to stay grounded and yet fired up for the game-day experience. I used an eclectic mix not many would associate with a pregame mixtape, but it worked for me. Groups like Blackfoot, INXS, Def Leppard, Madness, and Elton John headlined my chosen sounds.

I started the tape with Blackfoot's *Teenage Idol*. The song with a rocking beat told the story of a guy who wanted to become a rock star and left home but promised to come back when his goal was achieved. In a twist, I looked at this as an anthem of wanting to grow up and become a star for the team, not so much to become an individual idol per se. I wanted to do something worthy of becoming famous, not for personal gain but for the gain of the team and family and friends. (Keep humble—not for self, but for others.)

Next was Madness and their hit, *Our House*. The tag line, "Our house in the middle of the street," described our house in New Carrollton and all the good vibes that came from my days growing up in that special time and place. It reminded me of the safest time in my emotional life. Again, thinking of others and the true reason I wanted to achieve success, for the glory of God and my friends from the old neighborhood.

The tape continued with another Madness song, *Tomorrow's Just Another Day*. Again, aiming at keeping me humble in that no matter what happens today on the field, tomorrow will be another day. Don't get too high or too low with the ebb and flow of the game; it is only a game and tomorrow will come and life will move on.

Next, was an Elton John hit, *Don't Let the Sun Go Down on Me*. It spoke to me about needing to fight for what I wanted. "Don't let the sun go down on me; it would be like losing everything" the song states. I had to do my best not to let anything happen to my dream and stay focused when called on to do my job. Otherwise, I could lose everything, and the sun would go down on my dreams of bringing glory to God, my family, and friends.

Next, I threw in a song that will cause many reactions I'm sure, but being born and raised in the DC area, it became a dream that the Washington Redskins would need a kicker when Mark

Moseley retires, and I would be available for the job. That is what I kept telling myself. It was the Redskins fight song. It was more of a secondary dream of bringing honor to family and friends but also personal respect to my birthplace.

Next came INXS and their song *Don't Change*. Another going to the point of keeping me humble. "I'm standing here on the ground | The sky above won't fall down | See no evil in all directions | Resolution of happiness | Things have been dark for too long." These words painted a personal picture for me. I knew I had to keep my feet firmly on the ground, and by doing this, the sky wouldn't rain on my parade.

The evil I saw around my life during my high school years was gone, and I had resolved to find happiness all around me to keep the old darkness from my past at bay. No matter what happened during the year, I needed to stay the same person that I always have been and strive to be, who keeps humble and appreciates the life I have been given. IF I were to achieve success, I best not let it go to my head and become someone who I'm not.

Finally, the Def Leppard song *Rock of Ages* filled the role of a purely personal emotional fire-up tune if ever there was one. But a line in the song stood out to me: "It's better to burn out than fade away." This meant I needed to leave it all on the field that day, give it all I had, and not hold anything back for future endeavors. This resolution would prove vital in succeeding and thriving in the environment of college sports.

This collection of songs gained strength and meaning for me throughout the years, and to this day it reminds me of positive life qualities and life lessons I strive to live by daily. I could have chosen any number of songs, but I chose these with a purpose in mind—to stay humble and grounded in all I do.

Faith was another key component of my pregame routine. Like most aspects of my life, I kept this personal and quiet as well. The largest centering portion of my pregame routine came after the initial warm-up and final gathering of the team in the locker room. I would always seek some space away from the team in the back, away from others' routines. Before the coach's final talk prior to the game, I'd go to God in prayer and thank him for all his blessings and ask him to help me live to my potential to give him glory first. I would also lift my family, friends, and teammates in care and protection, and I continued to ask God to watch over my friend Marsha and help her heal and be truly successful.

I always included Marsha as a show of respect even when I lost track of her progress after her release from the hospital. I knew my life changed on the ski weekend I met her and then I decided to come to Adrian, and I always wanted to acknowledge God's direction and plan that brought me to this point. I will forever be grateful to Marsha for being part of God's plan in changing my outlook on life, but I felt bad that her negative health issues were the guides in my life. By praying for Marsha though, I always kept my eyes on others instead of on myself. This mindset has allowed me to be used by God in better ways and improved my outlook on life.

Life is such a fragile thing, but it also can be such a wonderful thing when we take the time to help and lift others. I would know when my heart was genuine and I was truly connected with God—he would send a tingle down my spine, which I'm sure was delivered directly through the Holy Spirit. I knew it was going to be unfair to the other team, but I relied on higher powers for any advantage I could get! Again, I am a kicker, not a stupid jock!

On my steps approach toward the kickoff, people in the

stands came to appreciate my creativity. I would curve like I was walking away from the ball then take off into a sprint straight on, strike the ball on the tee, and send it downfield. My parents heard some people talking with heightened anticipation before one of my kickoffs when one guy said to his friend, "Oh, you have to see this. It's like he sneaks up on the ball and blasts it downfield! Oh, yeah!" Sounds more like a wrestling interview, I know, but they enjoyed hearing it, and so did I.

My pregame and halftime ritual included being the last person in the locker room and the last one out. I used this time to continue to remind myself to stay humble and let others go before me. The game is not about me or my success, I am there to contribute to the team and glorify God's plan in my life. This ritual had a nice side benefit as well in that I didn't have to watch out for the other players stepping on my bare foot! It didn't matter who it was either, a freshman who had yet to play or the stars of the team. I knew what it was like to be at the bottom looking up and wanted to make sure my teammates felt respect before their opportunities to shine.

Finally, I had a routine my mom never fully appreciated: I refrained from getting a haircut during the football season. I had it cut just before camp and then after the season was over. I'm not sure of the reason behind this other than it was good enough for Sampson's strength in the Bible, so perhaps following that direction during the season would lead to supernatural strength for me. I must admit this, of all the rituals I carried out, was the pettiest to me, but who wants to mess with success after the sophomore season I had? Even if my mom was calling me Michelle by the end of that season with my long hair.

OFF-SEASON ACCOLADES

I honestly had no clue as to the off-season accolades I would be blessed with after my break-out season. I felt an internal peace about my efforts and had no expectations as to any personal rewards. Knowing our team had succeeded and I contributed to the success put me on an emotional high. Although I knew I had finished the year leading the nation in field goals made per game, what happened took me by surprise. I was blessed beyond belief with my first MIAA All-League Placekicker honor along with national recognition in earning the Pizza Hut Division III Honorable Mention All-American Placekicker.

My pregame prayer before the first game of the season was answered most spectacularly. God had helped me keep focused by staying humble and appreciative of all that surrounded me. This reinforced my faith in God's goodness towards me as well. I could not have achieved any of these accolades without the support of my teammates and in particular the guys on the special teams with me.

I specifically owed much of the year's success to Jeff and Steve, the other two members of our triad of place kicking—holder and long snapper—as well as all the guys who blocked on the line when I kicked. I shared my awards with all who had a direct hand in this success and all those behind the scenes supporting me—from family, friends and coaches to God's guidance and plan for my life. This was a year to remember and an awesome foundation for what the future had to hold. Bring on the next season!

— 13 —
Junior Year

— 13 —
Junior Year

The next season came with an expectation for greatness by everyone. The team was expected to go for the league championship, a national playoff invitation, and a national championship, not to mention my hopes for another nation-leading kicking statistic. Expectations are just that, dreams that require the matching actions to make them reality.

Unfortunatley, the team did not have the same cohesion as the previous year. That special spark we possessed the previous season just wasn't there. We were not at each other's throats bickering back and forth. That intangible magic, often described as "capturing lightning in a bottle," was just missing. Like someone had left the lid off our bottle this year.

Our field goal triad took on a new holder, Steve Konkle. The previous season, senior Jeff Hood did a fantastic job of holding the ball and keeping my head in the game. I am not a big fan of change, since Jeff graduated, I needed a new holder. Steve Konkle took on the task and executed it remarkably for the next two seasons. I didn't find out until years later this was his first experience in being a holder on any level. You want to talk about a wonderful master plan in action. I still had Steve Bohl as my long snapper, whose ability to expertly launch the ball back to us held my utmost confidence. This would prove to be an important and stable unit I would need to succeed.

We opened the season at home against Kenyon College, expecting to continue our dominant play from the playoff game of the previous season and take our place in history. The game did not go as expected. Though I was able to contribute with extra points and field goals, the game ended in the other team's favor. It was not like last year's magical first game. There was no celebration, no reporters wanting to interview us about the game, and no win. This set the season off on a different trajectory.

In the next game, we regrouped and looked more like the team we believed ourselves to be. We dominated in every aspect of the game and won 46–27. The season was about to turn around, and we would be back on track for our plans for a championship and making the playoffs.

The next game again showed the potential we had as a team and the results we expected with a 35–12 win against Ohio Northern. My leg got a good workout with several extra points and kickoffs kicked.

Next up was the perennial powerhouse, Mount Union College, from just outside of Akron, Ohio. This would be the strongest test for us of all the nonconference games. It was a hard-fought game as our teams were equally matched. I would take a more prominent role in this game in making a late-game field goal which put the game out of range for Mount Union to catch us with only a field goal. We won the game 31–27.

Homecoming against Alma came next on the schedule. Statistically, we dominated the game. Unfortunately, numbers on a sheet do not win games—the final score does—and we came up short, falling 14–27. This was not how we wanted to start league play. As the defending league champs, we were favored to win the conference again. But this year, the magic wasn't with us. We fought hard and still believed we could win each game but failed to put the complete game together.

The next week, we played our rival, Albion. We started the game strongly to lead 7–3 at the half. The second half didn't go our way with fumbles and interceptions during key drives. The final score ended up being 7–20.

Frustration with our ill fortune began to set in. Attesting to the team's character, there was no finger-pointing or blaming others; we just knew we were better than our record showed. I began doubting myself and my abilities and applied undue pressure on myself. I felt it was my duty to help lead the team as I had last year, but I was not given as many chances as I had that season.

I couldn't understand why I wasn't leading the nation again and asked to meet with the coach to find out what could be done. I wasn't expecting his response when I told him I was in a funk about the year. Coach Labadie delivered a tough explanation, putting it back on me and said it was all in my head. I was experiencing a rut and needed to figure it out myself.

At first, I was confused. I did not get an answer to how I could fix things so we would be leading the league and nation again. I left the meeting believing it was all my fault the team was not as successful this season. Though this was not true, it did get me to think deeply about the situation.

I realized dark forces were attacking me and sowing self-doubt to bring me back to old selfish thoughts from high school. Fortunately, I was stronger now and began to realize the best solution was to go back to the beginning and understand the positive thoughts that got me to this place. Look for the positive and build on that.

So, that is what I did. I went back and threw out the doubt

and negativity and began to look at the little things that I was doing well and build on my success. I began with more attention to extra points. I spent more time perfecting my approach and technique during practice. I also began to think about how I can help others, focusing outward rather than on myself. A little reminder now and again does not hurt.

We could turn our fortunes around the next week against Hope. The game started rather lopsided with Hope going up 17–0. I kicked a field goal before halftime for a 17–3 score. Hope scored again to make it 24–3 before we changed the momentum and scored twice to cut the deficit to 24–17.

We had the momentum, but Hope ended up making a spectacular play with a 64-yard touchdown that put the game out of reach. The final score of 38–17 didn't reflect the closeness of the game, but I felt better about my performance and knew our team still had some fight.

Mathematically, we were out of the hunt for the league championship, but we had a strong desire to end the year strong to build for next year. Olivet fell next on the schedule. We put together the quintessential perfect game and set league records in rushing and total offense. The defense recorded a shutout and special teams did their job for a total team victory, 66–0. We finally reflected the team we had believed we were at the start of the season.

Kalamazoo was our next target, and our team delivered another inspiring game. The final score of 31–0 showed our team coming into its own. Two strong games in a row, our dominant defense showed its strength. I felt good about my contribution to the team but also that I had more to give next year.

I ended the year making 30 of 30 extra-point attempts and 5

of 8 field goals. I had no tackles this year, but there were no kick-off returns for touchdowns against us either. I was again honored with the MIAA First-Team Kicker designation but did not earn national awards. I knew I hadn't done anything to earn national recognition this season, but knowing the feeling from last year, I vowed to train and practice to put myself in a position to earn something next season.

— 14 —
The Final Season

— 14 —
The Final Season

My senior year was full of personal expectations. I wanted to do my best and start strong to wipe the previous year off my mind. I wanted to get back to leading the nation and helping the team get back to the playoffs.

To hit these goals, I needed to focus on being a good teammate and doing my best as a part of the total team effort. This was another year to focus on being humble and not taking my post-season accolades too seriously. The summer before, I resumed training hard to get into the best shape I could before football training camp.

The year began with a local youth fan, Terry, coming by practice to help in shagging footballs and doing more to help the team. Terry became more comfortable with the team, and the coaches and team accepted him as a member of the support staff. You could see his confidence grow through the year.

He began to hang around campus after practice and even brought his new girlfriend to meet me. It was with a sense of pride he was able to introduce her to a member of the team, and I was happy to validate him. It was getting late and since it was getting dark and I didn't want them to be walking back, I offered to drive them home. I could tell this was another point of pride for Terry and helped to build his self-esteem.

Through the year I took him to his home several more times and was able to talk about the future—his future—and to give him some positive uplifting praise in hopes that this would make a difference in his life. In many ways, I saw myself in him and knew if I had a head start of someone giving me advice, I may have had an easier time turning the corner of self-esteem issues.

You could tell we were quietly feeling confident about our chances this year. Everyone was working hard and had a renewed desire to return to the winning ways of our league championship. We came out strong in the first game against Kenyon with a convincing 34–6 victory. I was able to contribute to the team's victory. We started strong, and I could tell this was going to be a good year for everyone.

The next week we traveled to Heidelburg College. This game started with an injury I had not experienced since childhood. During the pregame warmups, I somehow stepped on a bee which stung my bare foot. It didn't physically bother me to the point of too much pain, but I did keep an extra eye out for clover patches and additional danger.

As it was, we became involved in a close game and were ahead at one point, 14–3. Unfortunately, we were not able to hold the opponent this time and ended up losing 15–14. A tough loss, but nothing that would stop us from winning the league, so we would press on.

Next, we took on Ohio Northern and won convincingly, 42–0. My leg was fatigued from all the extra points and kickoffs. Taking part in that victory kept me focused and positive about my contribution and our team's chances for reaching our goals.

A game early in the season was a road trip to Mount Union outside Akron, Ohio. I looked forward to it for several reasons. Mount Union's strong team would test our resolve, but it would also be a reunion. My New Carrollton gang was coming to see me play. I was so excited for this game and wanted to do my best for the guys. My mom set everything in motion with the Lamb family and made hotel reservations to stay after the game.

The game was close with a final score of 20–16. We lost that game, and I didn't have as many opportunities as I had hoped. I did kick a few extra points and attempted a field goal but pulled it to the left in a close miss. What I valued the most about that game was my neighbor Dave's banner with his artwork that he attached to the fence behind our bench to encourage me. I carefully removed it after the game and kept it in my memory vault. I still have it to this day!

It was an awesome feeling to have them there, and it turned out they were the only non-Adrian College friends who saw me play in an actual game. This meant so much to me that they made the effort to come to see me play. This is why I say, they may have been friends but are truly family in my eyes. It was good for my spirit to see everyone and reminisce about old times and have a couple of meals together before we all had to return home the next day. I was humbled and so happy to have them there.

We came back the next week to start league play against Olivet College, our last homecoming as seniors. We knew focusing on league play was the best chance to achieve a high goal for the season. We wanted to take back the league crown we were striving for. The team worked hard and pulled together a great win, 49–0.

Next, we played our then-archrival Hope College in Holland, Michigan. This game took on special significance due to a pro football strike that year. Our contest made history as the first NCAA Division III football game to be televised live in the state of Michigan. With play full of heart on both sides, we ultimately came out on top, 21–14. Making three extra points in the game,

I later found out my extra-point streak was the topic of conversation among the announcers during the game. I was fortunate to secure a copy of the telecast and view the game from a different perspective. It was the first time Hope had lost a homecoming game in twenty years, and the first loss they had in that stadium in four years. A total team effort gave us hope for another league championship.

Ironically, it was around that time my coaches began to talk about the streak I was amassing and mentioned I was possibly in line for the Division III consecutive–extra-point streak. My coaches didn't make much of it at the time; it was mentioned more in passing at practice at first. They said they were having to do some additional research about it, but I had a nice streak going. That was all I heard from them about it until the final game of the season.

Alma was our next opponent, and pre-season rankings picked them to win the league that year. They were a good team, but their 0–2 record did not reflect their talent. We were talented too, and that day we put together a game that hit on all cylinders. We won 70–6, another tiring day for me with so many extra points and kickoffs. Our team was becoming the dominant force we believed we could be.

Now it was on to the next opponent. Our next big game was against Albion College was unique since it was a fellow United Methodist–supported college. I was all for the friendly rivalries many of our MIAA opponents provided.

I found out some pregame insider knowledge from my dorm neighbor Charlie close to game day. Charlie had traveled to a volleyball game to watch his sister Rose play. Sitting in the stands rather incognito, he happened to sit a few rows down from many of the football players taking in the volleyball match after their practice. The conversations between the teammates caught Charlie's attention as they had to do with the team strategy to beat Adrian the upcoming weekend.

Surprisingly, Charlie heard my name mentioned in their strategy. He took note and kind of chuckled to himself. They planned to block one of my extra points. Their coaches thought it would devastate me and the team if they could break my streak. They hoped it would rattle me so that if the game came down to a game-winning field goal, I would be an emotional wreck, unable to make that game-winning kick!

Charlie returned to our dorm after the match and sought me out to relay the story to me and some of the other guys in the hallway. All the guys, including myself, burst out in laughter as Charlie told us about their grand desire to block one of my extra points.

I honestly didn't know what to think. I had never thought much about my streak up to that point and didn't focus on the fact that I had never missed an extra point. I realized that my desire to stay humble and not look at the individual accolades—or at least not dwell on things until after the season—kept me from obsessing. This news made me aware how special the streak was and how others were taking note and believed it was a legitimate attack strategy.

The fact that another coaching staff believed my consecutive–extra-point streak was worth targeting was completely comical to me at the time. I knew I couldn't dwell on this strategy or let it get into my head. I remember going forward in practice, making sure I took a little extra time on my extra points, keeping the same swing as always, and getting the ball up quickly to stay out of reach of any potential blocks.

When game time arrived, I was able to focus and go about my duties. I kicked two field goals and an extra point that day, but we ended up losing 20–13. It was a hard fought game and had a twist we couldn't see coming. During the game, Steve Konkle drew a flag and was thrown out of the game. I'm not sure the exact reasoning or how it was instigated against him, all I knew is there goes my holder! What was going to happen next? The back up holder was called to take some practice snaps on the sidelines. Charlie Otlewski was a sophmore at the time and was well aware of the streak I had and was called on to hold for the extra point that day. I could tell he was nervous, and I tried to encourage him as Jeff had spoken to me when I was a sophomore and told him we can do this. Coach sent us out to kick the extra point and delivered a special message to Charlie as he was running out on the field " don't screw it up". The kick went off perfectly and Charlie had done a good job - we made the extra point. I'm not sure who was more relieved that day, but Charlie had the weight of the world lifted off him for sure!

Albion didn't block any of my kicks that day. I would come to see they just couldn't mess with divine intervention. Too many mistakes as a team and turnovers appeared to derail our opportunity for another league championship. How we would respond to this setback would testify to our team's resolve.

Our last bit of hope for winning the league championship was that Albion would lose the next week and we would take care of business with Kalamazoo. God had a plan, but we had to do our part.

It was ridiculous how many special things happened during the final game of the season and my career at Adrian. We played against Kalamazoo as heavy favorites. During the week, Coach Lyall pressed us to practice a special play which had never been used in the last three years. We have been practicing it since my sophmore year. Perhaps they worried the fake extra-point/field-goal kicker option might endanger my foot, being barefoot and all. Or maybe they just had more confidence in their other proven fake play.

The play was rather simple. Steve Konkle, the holder, received the ball from Steve Bohl, the long snapper. When the ball was snapped, Konkle stood up to reverse pivot and run to the right of the line, while I followed in an arc a few yards to the side of him. Steve's responsibility was to check for any close defenders and shoot through the line if there was an opening. Otherwise, he would turn and pitch the ball to me, and it was my job to run the ball into the end zone.

We ran it several times during practice for Coach Labadie, who just shook his head, as he had the previous three years. But this time he relented, saying if we were up by four scores, we would run it. A ray of hope existed. Excitement and nerves hit me all at once.

Would anyone target my foot? Would I be able to run fast enough to get across the line? Would I be able to take a hit when everyone could legally target a kicker? I might get the answer to all these questions the next Saturday afternoon at our home stadium.

Just don't screw it up! I thought.

The game started, and we quickly scored. I came in to kick the first extra point and made it. I remember wanting to go out in style. I always tried to kick the ball over the fence that lined the stadium on either end of the field. I would often play this little joyful in-game activity in my mind. It had been a long season, and my leg was feeling some fatigue, but the surge of adrenaline from being on the home field for the last time propelled me to kick it over the fence. I also made a second successful attempt that day.

We scored a third touchdown, and I was called on to kick yet another extra point, though I didn't know it would be the last one I kicked for Adrian. The snap came back to Steve as it always had, and he placed it on the tee as usual, but the unthinkable happened. The ball slipped off the tee!

I was about to panic and hesitated slightly. I didn't hear Steve call "fire," which would set into motion a designed play to abort the kick. He would then throw a pass to one of the players who, released from blocking, would get to a designated spot where the ball could be thrown to one.

After my heart stopped for a brief moment, I continued with the kick and made contact with the ball. Panic poured across my mind thinking, I shouldn't have done that, I should have made the "fire" call myself! I remember peeking up and finding the ball floating like a wounded duck floating through the air. It seemed to move in slow motion, wobbling just over the crossbar but most importantly between the uprights—the kick was good!

Konkle congratulated me as he usually did after each kick, but this time he also profusely apologized for the ball slipping off the tee and not calling to abort. I laughed and reassured him, "It's ok; we made the kick. No harm done."

My heart began to beat again, and the adrenaline rush began to bring life back to my face, I'm sure. After I thanked the guys on the line for blocking and Bohl for his good snap, I trotted toward the sideline. I also realized there is no way I would have made that kick if I was used to a two-inch tee—thank you, Eddie Murray, for the advice to go to a one-inch tee back in high school! And thank God for a little divine help in giving me a calm disposition that didn't get rattled when things went a little wonky.

Adrian was comfortably up 21–0, and my anticipation heightened that the coach was going to let us run the kicker option play after the next score. As I ran off the field, I was greeted by Coach Labadie, and he was peeling back his headset and microphone communicator to tell me, "Nice kick, but you didn't get the national record after all. There is a kid out in Iowa who has a longer streak."

Well, how do you like that? Just about missed the extra point and now learned I missed out on a record. A little deflating to say the least, but I still had a job to do in the kickoff. I took this frustration and funneled it into the kick after that. I don't remember much about how far it went, but I do remember the satisfaction of releasing the frustration into the kickoff. I went back to the sidelines to join my teammates, and Konkle again sought me out to apologize. I just laughed it off and reminded him we made it, so all is good. It's most helpful to look on the bright side of any situation, even when it doesn't go according to my plan . . . after all, it is part of God's plan.

Stay on an even keel . . . don't get too high or too low in your emotions if you want to be a success. True, it was a close call, but there was something special about that kick, and I knew I was one fortunate kicker.

The game progressed, and the defense held tough again. It was time for the offense to take over. They moved down the field with a precision that resulted in yet another touchdown. I had my tee in hand and was ready to run on for another extra point when

I heard the coach smile and give us the go-ahead for the "kicker option."

I set up as usual, and the team huddled to call the play. Konkle looked back at me and asked if I was ready. I nodded and said, "Let's do this."

Konkle's hands went up to accept the snap from Bohl, and the command came out "Fire . . . Fire . . . Fire." Konkle stood up and made his pivot; I pushed off and arced around him in my bare foot and shoe. It looked like a mass of confusion I had never experienced before.

I saw an opening form with the perfect execution of the blocking scheme by the right side of the front line. The hole was wide enough a car could have driven through it and not touched anyone. I figured Konkle would run it in with ease, which he could have, but instead, he turned and pitched the ball to me!

Panic set in, and I knew there was only one conclusion to this play that would satisfy everyone—I had to get across the end line. I got the ball and covered it with both arms like the running back drills I followed during camp. I saw the opening slowly collapsing and decided the only way to make it was to dive for the endzone. From about to the two-yard line I dove forward to get the ball across the line. My mind whirled with so many thoughts: I hope no one steps on my exposed foot; I hope I make it; I want to provide a spark for the team.

I felt a few opponents slam into me as I dove, and I looked around and saw the line at my waist, the ball safe and secure in the endzone. I had done it, my first—and only—two-point conversion!

The home crowd erupted, and the team enthusiastically congratulated me as we left the field. I was congratulating them on

117

their blocking, snapping, and pitch and knew this was the end of the line for me.

I felt elated and so proud of the team for being able to pull off this play. I was also so appreciative of Konkle for making the pitch to me when he honestly could have walked it into the end-zone if he wanted. He told me "There is no way I was going to run it in myself, I wanted Mike to feel how it felt to make it to the endzone." I appreciated the opportunity and thanked him.

I came off the field to an enthusiastic Coach Lyall who was jumping and high-fiving everyone as they came to the sidelines. He then gave me my high five and a huge smile, congratulating me on the successful conclusion of the infamous "kicker option." Coach Labadie tried to get the extra-point team off the field so we didn't get a delay of game penalty, but he couldn't hold back a sly smile and gave his congratulations to us for our conversion.

Coach Labadie then directed me to head to the sidelines to let the other kickers get some work. I knew that moment was the fitting end to my kicking career at Adrian. I was elated and deflated all at once. The team members took their turns stopping by to congratulate me on the play and the amazing career.

As I stood on the sidelines, I took everything in and took my turn making the rounds to show my appreciation to the guys on the team, especially the seniors who traveled the journey together as brothers in the great game of football. I was humbled at the opportunity I had to play the game and the experiences I had gone through.

The crowd in the stands yelled their congratulations to me as well, and I shyly acknowledged with a wave and a smile. I looked into the stands to find my parents, and they gave their smiles and waves in a job well done as well.

Eventually, I was approached by two young fans who came down to the railing behind the bench and asked for my autograph. This took me by surprise, but instead of fulfilling their request, I told them I couldn't during the game. Of all the things I look back on in my career, this was surely the one regret I had about that senior year. It was an honor to be the kicker for Adrian College and to perform for all who came to our games over the years. I wanted to bring joy to all, not boost myself.

I justified my response because I didn't want to get a big head. I wanted to stay humble about the whole situation. I also didn't want the rest of the team to get the wrong idea that I had let things go to my head after all. But in the end, I received a simple request from a child and didn't fulfill it.

I had never been approached for my autograph before and didn't know the proper protocol for the situation. If I had it to do over again, I should have told them to come to see me after the game or just signed it quickly and went about the rest of the game rooting for my teammates. It has honestly bothered me for years, and I just hope the kids understood and didn't hold it against me as I have regretted it all these years.

The journey started with me being the only player not to play a single play on varsity my freshman year while trying out a new barefoot kicking style. It progressed to having the opportunity to start my second year. I ended up leading the nation and being an integral part of the team that made it to the national playoffs for the first time in program history. The ups and downs of being a kicker in the collegiate ranks had wild emotional swings I tried to keep in check on my outward demeanor.

The season ended that day for us as we fell short of our goal to make it back to the playoffs. It was rather surreal as fans poured

119

onto the field to congratulate the participants and socialize per tradition after the game. Knowing it was the last time we would be assembled as a team on the field of play gave me a sense of pride in being a part of a program in college football that started close to 100 years prior.

Being a part of something truly greater than my individual effort and knowing I gave my all to make the team better, generated satisfaction and a sense of belonging I could only compare to my days in New Carrollton and the family of friends there. I knew being a part of this team was special in so many ways, a journey truly designed for me by a higher presence than myself.

— 15 —
College Life Confidence

— 15 —
College Life Confidence

Contrary to popular belief, you cannot major in football in college. Adrian had a strong liberal arts program, and the school was well known for its business program. I majored in business management. The department had a cohesive teaching crew with a great mix of real-life experience and relatable personalities which displayed care for educating its students. During my four years at Adrian, our class developed a special relationship with the teaching staff. I had a good relationship with all of the teachers—from the department head, Mr. Bachman, to the marketing guru, Mr. Quinlan.

Mr. Bachman had a reputation as a strict teacher who was difficult to communicate with. I had him for some preliminary management classes early in my college career, and he lived up to the intimidating persona in class. It wasn't until my internship during my junior-year summer break that I began to understand his demeanor and business face.

I believe people come into our lives with a purpose and plan to enrich our lives if we let them. I began to better understand the department and the real-world concepts they taught us through our class studies and projects. They brought us along and taught us to work as a team but to continue to have confidence in our thoughts and beliefs when it comes to business matters. We learned the key to dealing with others is firmness and confidence in your convictions.

One senior class requirement, Strategic Business, had a reputation of being the most difficult class. As luck would have it, I was chosen to instead participate in a special class that would be taught by an outside professor, exempting me from the Strategic Business course. Not a bad gig. I had no idea who the teacher was going to be, but it couldn't be any more intimidating than all I had heard about the alternative. I knew most of the people in this class, and many were athletes who performed at high levels in their respective sports or were high achievers in the business department.

The new professor was announced as Mr. Gar Laux, the former vice-chairman and VP of Sales and Marketing at Chrysler, VP of Ford, and a major part of the Mustang project team with Lee Iacocca. So much for being less intimidating than Mr. Bachman—this professor was a world-class leader in the business world!

Mr. Laux's approach to teaching came at information from a business angle rather than a teaching angle. Mr. Laux gave us opportunities to learn in ways we would soon experience in the real world. The course emphasized teamwork and communication to develop important skills we would need as we moved into our professions the following year. The most amazing skill he demonstrated was reading the room and each of his students easily and accurately and bringing out the best in us.

Our projects included field trips to manufacturing facilities including Chrysler assembly plants, high-powered marketing agencies, automotive supplier manufacturing plants, and we even tapped into our own college experience. One out-of-the-box exercise challenged the class to come up with ideas for the restoration of Ellis Island that were then sent directly to Mr. Laux's friend, Lee Iacocca, who at the time was in charge of the Ellis Island restoration program.

This class probably developed me and my confidence levels more than any other class I took at Adrian. He took the time to find out about each student. It wasn't long before I was being chided and congratulated about my achievements on the football field by Mr. Laux, especially about playing without footwear.

Learning that I was a fan of the Washington Redskins from growing up in the DC area, Mr. Laux took the time to contact Coach George Allen Sr., his personal friend and a former head coach of the Redskins. Coach Allen sent me an autographed poster with a personal note I will always cherish. Mr. Laux took the time to get to know each of us and personalize our education in ways other professors would never be able to achieve. It was one of the reasons everyone from that class went on to have amazing careers after school. Our interactions with him provided a unique perspective to make the business world a better place.

As the semester continued, we were challenged to come up with all the problems we saw with the college and write a paper on these issues. The class was broken up into teams, with fellow football teammates and I taking on the campus facilities. Just as we were about to turn in the finished product, Mr. Laux told us we would be making a presentation to the president of the college himself! This new aspect of the evaluation taught us to have confidence in our abilities and not be intimidated by the status of who we were presenting any project to.

The second semester of the class was built around providing solutions to the issues we developed in the first semester. We learned it was easy to come up with the problems but always follow up with solutions, especially when making presentations to those in higher authority. This lesson stayed with me through my postcollege career.

In the end, one of the greatest gifts Mr. Laux provided me was a gift of critique on my class participation. He said I was a quiet person that had much to offer any organization, and I should be sure to speak up and share my knowledge and move the team forward. We all have something to offer this world, and we should not be afraid to dive in and make the world a better place. As I got to know Mr. Laux over that year, I understood his teaching was driven by a desire to pass along his years of tactical and strategic wisdom and his many valuable life lessons of how to respect others' unique talents.

Friendship

The cornerstone of my success lay in God's plan for my life. He completed the process with unique experiences, fantastic professors, amazingly talented teammates, and coaches as strong building blocks for the journey. He also provided me with the most special friends along the way to keep me grounded and traveling on the road he designed for me. I started life with amazing friends in New Carrollton who continue to be truly like family to me. He also sprinkled in friendships that have stood the test of time along the way. In college, he blessed me with a new crop of friends who again have become like family as well.

My life took a dark turn when I was in high school, and I was convinced I would never have friends. In fact, I believed I didn't need friends to get through life. I was going down a dark, lonely tunnel that had no end in sight. The fact is, the light at the end of the tunnel was a train coming straight at me, and I didn't even recognize the danger.

125

Many people in life feel they don't need friends or anyone in their life to get through this journey. I know—I was one of them at one time. I can also admit, I was wrong. Almost dead wrong. The truth of the matter is, God made us communal beings, meaning we need human contact, to receive help from and to help others.

All lives are special in so many ways, and the road map of life has many stops and many people along the way. Some people come into our lives briefly, perhaps only a couple of hours, and make a significant impact. (Thank you, Eddie Murray, for your wisdom to use a shorter tee.) Others impact you for half a decade or more. (Thank you, New Carrollton friends/family.) God placed people in my life when I needed them most, and some I didn't recognize until it was too late, but they had a purpose in my growth as well.

I had a group of friends at Adrian who became family as well. My roommate Bill became like a brother to me. My good friend Gina offered great support in all my efforts in sports and school. CW opened my eyes to view the world differently and inspired me to strive to be a better version of myself. Mary Beth became my first long-term girlfriend and major support; she helped me come out of my shell. The freshman dorm crew from Davis Hall, the corridor mates from Estes Hall and our intramural teams known as the Gators fed my daily social life. Tami helped me find my future family, and my classmates supported each other and presented alternatives for the future of Adrian College in Mr. Laux's class.

These were the main characters in my life, not including all the supporting cast who made me a better version of myself. We have a close and supportive graduating class, and I give thanks for each of them as we meet at reunions, remember the past, and support each other more in future needs.

God has a gift and a purpose for each one of us as well. You may be on a special mission in life that will affect the whole world or perhaps one person's world. You may be the catalyst that causes a chain reaction that will affect many others or a special other person. Never doubt that you were sent here for a purpose. Sometimes you need to listen for a long time for that purpose. Sometimes you need to listen intensely to find your purpose. Either way, you need to listen; why else would you be given two ears and one mouth? To listen twice as much as you talk.

Having a friend comes most when you become a friend, when you are thinking of others rather than wrapped up in yourself and your issues and problems. When you humble yourself and have a servant's heart, you can build the team God has planned for you to get through the journey of life more enjoyably, the way God intended it to be.

— 16 —
Not the End

— 16 —
Not the End

There were many life lessons I was lovingly guided through during the many highs and lows I experienced. Many items come to mind and several life lessons I have been blessed in understanding. I've been able to study many of these and would like to share some of them with you in hopes you can use some to enhance your life and the lives of those around you. I call them the "Farrell 15" in honor of my jersey number in college. Why didn't I have a single-digit jersey like most kickers? It wasn't part of the plan!

The collegiate kicking story is over, but not my amazing life story. The journey that is my life has gone through many twists and turns; many I would not have chosen for myself if it were up to me. Thankfully, God's plan for my life was perfect to achieve the outcome for this less-than-perfect individual. Staying humble and seeking accolades not for myself but for those around me and those looking on was the only way to follow the ultimate plan. Patience and perseverance were key components as well.

My accolades continued after my college career ended. Locally I earned my third First-Team All MIAA placekicker honor and set a modern day league record for points after touchdowns. A second Special Teams Player of the Year award from the team. A Second Team All-American award surprised me tremendously, at that point the highest athletic honor any football player had earned in the program history.

During the end-of-the-year banquet, it was mentioned I had

completed my career with an astounding 84-of-84 perfect completion record on my extra-point kicks, with 3 for 3 during the playoffs. This was believed to be a new team record and possible MIAA record. A few weeks later I was also told I was the only kicker in the history of Division III football to make all my extra points based on at least eighty attempts!

This honor did not immediately register with me. I was PERFECT in my attempts. God had taken an imperfect person and made something perfect. I knew it couldn't have been by my athletic abilities alone. It truly had to be God directed! The last time I missed an extra point in a college stadium was during the University of Michigan Kicking School in "The Big House"!

Why did God grace me with this honor? I may never know in this lifetime, but I am truly thankful. I was always told records were made to be broken. But this one will never be! You cannot get higher than 100%; it will only be tied from here on out! That alone is the most humbling sentiment of all. If it wasn't for the work of my teammates and me working together, this would never have happened. My name is the one mentioned, but I had so much help from my teammates and support around me.

God gave me options. Sometimes the options I chose veered me away from his ultimate plan for my life. Fortunately, God was gracious enough to give me other options that brought me back in line with this plan. God wants us to succeed. Like a caring earthly parent who will move mountains for the success of their children, God moved mountains for me to succeed beyond any of my expectations.

I know I am not the first or the only person God has delivered supernatural success to, and his guidance can be achieved by you who read this now. Humble your heart, listen for direction, and follow what you know to be truly from God. The journey is a long process and success is available to everyone, just not usually overnight. Then again, anything is possible with God. Second, third, and fourth chances abound, and double digits are available if truly needed. God has a success plan available for every one of our lives, and it is available for receiving and always given freely. I caution you not to expect success quickly as time has no control over the Master Plan. No matter what your station is in life right now, success is available for your future.

My life journey was filled with options. I could choose to play football or not. I could

choose to punt or placekick. I could choose to use the two-inch tee or the one-inch tee. I could choose to kick with a shoe or without. I could choose to go to Adrian College or any other school. I could choose to stay at Adrian College after not playing freshman year or transfer to another school to try and play. I could choose to cave in or fight for the kicking job when faced with overwhelming competition. I could choose to listen to the other team's plans to derail my record attempt or block it out and do my job. I could choose to be boastful and dismissive of others and claim greatness for myself, or I could be humble and faithful in my pursuit to esteem others. I can choose to follow God's plan for my life or take my own route, and you have the same option! Never give up on whatever you do, and keep kicking. With or without a shoe, it truly is your choice.

PATIENCE LESSONS CONTINUE . . .

All of these awards were a great honor and a special way to cap off an amazing career. A coveted honor was further into the future though. You see, God is not done with me yet and still has life lessons to teach me.

I hoped to become a part of the permanent athletics honors in the Hall of Fame one day. I believed my efforts and recognitions deserved inclusion, and I wanted the opportunity to thank so many people who supported my journey. My parents and brother came to mind first. Always there, they gave me unwavering support in all I accomplished in life.

The friends I found at Adrian College supported my journey and became some of my closest friends in life and deserve so much appreciation for being true friends and keeping me grounded during this amazing journey. My family of friends in Maryland will always be the inspiration that began my journey. My friends in Fenton supported me through the high school years and beyond. And my coaches and teammates gave me constant support on the field and off.

Every five years I attend our class reunion. I always look forward to this time to reminisce, catch up, and continue to grow the relationships that originated at Adrian. I stop by and talk to my former coaches, support staff in athletics, and professors in the business department.

I felt induction into the Hall of Fame would give me a chance to thank them all publicly, so they could have on-record how much I appreciated them all. But this would not play out as I had hoped.

I would be first eligible for the Hall of Fame ten years after graduation, but it wasn't God's plan for me then. Year after year, I waited patiently to no avail. Over and over, I witnessed friends receive induction to the Hall of Fame. They were each worthy for inclusion into the Hall of Fame, but few held the number of national or team records I had to my credit.

I wondered, Was this some form of "kicker persecution" I was receiving or some other unexplained bias? Frustrating as it was, I had to live with not becoming a member of Adrian's Hall of Fame. I fueled inside jokes between my friends and I—I didn't have a chance because I was not a multi-sport athlete, and a "non-athlete" kicker didn't check off the right boxes. It would turn out to be more of a lesson from God in patience.

The year 1996 came and went with no call. For eleven consecutive years, I waited and watched each announcement, but no joy for me. For many years I felt pain, confusion, disrespect, and bitterness because I thought I should be included.

Then in 1998, a tragedy occurred when my mom suddenly died. As a self-admitted "mama's boy," I was devastated. I wanted my mother to be a part of the ceremony to honor her support of my playing days. I felt lost and wondered why God took my mom before she had a chance to be a part of the celebration. I honestly was in a funk and felt a deep disappointment with my biggest supporter out of the picture. For several years, I honestly lost interest in being inducted into the Hall as I wallowed in my loss.

About five years later, it came to me that my feelings—or lack of feelings—for getting into the Hall of Fame went against everything I had built up during my collegiate run. For years I would return to the campus for the homecoming festivities and congratulate those being inducted into the Hall, many from my graduating class. We had a great class evidenced by all the people who were eventually inducted into Adrian's Athletic Hall of Fame. It became rather comical to me that I would wish several inductees my congratulations and they would ask what year I had been inducted. Their reactions of course were comforting to me in their amazement that I was not in already, but I always had the blind faith it would happen for me eventually.

I began to spiral into believing those were nice sentiments, but this special recognition would not become a reality. Why didn't God's plan include recognizing my accomplishments? What was I missing? Has something gone against my mojo during my kicking career?

That's when it hit me—I was wanting this too much for myself and not as a vehicle for others to join the party. It took me a few years to cleanse my system and get in touch with the new way of thinking, but I began to feel the tingle in my spine and knew I was on the right track.

The year 2008 was different. I was invited to be part of a special ceremony for our whole 1983 football team's induction into the Hall of Fame celebrating our league championship and first-ever playoff appearance.

There were many people I wanted to stop by to see and thank before the ceremonial walk through campus and the official start of the ceremony. As luck would have it, I did not schedule my visits well and missed the ceremonial walk through campus, joining the festivities at the dining hall where our dinner was to take place. The dining hall was quite full with the large number of inductees and families in attendance.

The ceremony brought back memories from our special season, the struggles and successes we had back in the day. We were able to reminisce with the coaches and fellow players at the dinner held to celebrate the inductees. It was a good feeling to be recognized with our team and even to receive individual recognition during the coach's acceptance speech for the significant contributions my kicking made that year. This was the feeling of pride I imagined it would feel like to be part of the Hall of Fame— along with the knowledge my mom and others who had passed previous to the induction shared in the sense of accomplishment.

God gave me a lesson about patience. Time gives us a perspective that teaches events to happen on his time, not ours. In fact, his plan is usually better and bigger than anything we can imagine when we follow it. This story was not over—God had more blessings to bestow.

The next chapter in God's plan even topped the previous year. In 2009 I received a call from Coach Riley, the chair of the Hall of Fame committee, informing me I had been elected individually to the Hall of Fame for the next class! I was overwhelmed and humbled again. He said he would follow up with a letter discussing more of the details and completed the call mentioning I would need to develop a five- to seven-minute acceptance speech. This culminated the roller coaster of high and low emotions which had not culminated until I humbled myself and recognized that mine was a recognition of the total team effort and the support I received from family and friends outside the team.

The speech took front and center in my mind. All my childhood anxieties for public speaking began to bubble up inside me and clash with my desire to properly thank everyone who was a part of this journey. I knew I had to ask for help and prayed for guidance in developing the speech.

At the end of an interview spot on radio my sophomore year, the interviewer ended it commenting that I was a man of few words and let my kicking do the talking for me from the field. I would not have this issue twenty-two years later. God helped me overcome my shyness and gifted me a writing ability that filled page after page of a speech. The kicker had something to say, and people needed to hear it!

When my practice speeches were running north of thirty minutes, I began to worry. I was able to trim the speech down, but knew it would run over the three- to five-minute suggestion I received. However, I had peace that there were many that needed to be lifted, so I pressed on.

The weekend finally arrived, and I felt strangely similar to game day. What did I do on this game day at Adrian? You guessed it—I shaved my foot and added some cologne just as I had done many years before. Anxiousness and excitement defined the day. About twenty-five people were attending the ceremony with direct ties to me, an honor in its own right. I knew I had to be strong for all those in attendance. Here was my chance to thank them directly like I never had before.

My wife and kids were also able to attend. They had not seen me in this environment before and enjoyed the attention from and communion with my friends and family. My then eight-year-old son, David, and my four-year-old daughter, Mae, had become the center of my universe. Their unique personalities and excitement only added to the joyful weekend celebration, making it even more special for me.

Friday morning we shared a special moment. I got a bag of footballs from the team supplies, and they watched me kick on the football field with my signature barefoot style. I remember the bulldog mascot was a particular favorite of David's, and he would hug on the costumed person throughout the day. Mae found the large dog costume a bit frightening and sought me out to pick her up when the bulldog came around.

The night began with the Bulldog Walk from the student center through campus to the dining hall where the ceremony would take place (which I had missed the year before). Current athletes lined the sidewalk and cheered all the inductees. Our families met us at the end of the line, but my Mae couldn't wait. Seeing me walking down the sidewalk, she took off for me from twenty feet down the sidewalk and latched onto my leg in one of the cutest expressions of affection I had ever experienced. She accompanied me to the end of the line before the rest of my family pulled her aside as we passed them.

When dinner was served, my family had three tables full of support. I was in awe that so many came to share this time with me. My strong support group made up one of the largest contingents that night. Time slowed as I glanced around and looked at everyone, and memories replayed and danced in my mind. I was so grateful for their presence there that night and throughout my life. They came from far and near—Texas, Missouri, Kansas, Georgia, Michigan, and South Carolina—to be part of this occasion.

I finally had this special time to show them my appreciation. With dinner complete, the introductions and speeches began. I was in the middle of the pack for my turn, and honestly, the night became a blur to me at this point.

I heard my name called to take the podium. I remember walking up to the stage during a pleasant round of applause. I got to the podium and looked around and drank in the sea of people now fixated on what I was about to say. It was a bit intimidating to say the least. I started my speech then stopped after my initial appreciation remarks to do what I normally did during a football game. I excused myself and took off my right shoe. (I left the sock on—it was a formal event mind you!)

With a sigh of relief, I told the room I wasn't used to performing at Adrian in front of this many people without my shoe off. This drew a laugh from the crowd and in turn shattered the walls of my anxieties. Then I could begin with the confidence and the will to make all the necessary thanks to those in attendance as well as those not able to attend. This most heartfelt speech of my life took the most time of any inductee that night and possibly the history of the ceremonies! I'm not sure exactly how long I spoke, but I'm sure I went over by several minutes.

There was another round of applause as I walked down to my seat and most of the room stood. As I walked down the steps with one shoe off and turned the corner of the tables, Mae greeted me again, jumping from her chair to hug my leg tightly again. Wrapped around my leg, she escorted me back to the table where I received additional congratulations from the friends and family who attended to support me. I admit though, I remember little to nothing after I took off my shoe. I can only believe the Holy Spirit took over for me in my speech. I knew I had a peaceful feeling about what I spoke, thanking all who were such a big part of my success.

God still has a plan for my life and always will. I realized quickly after the celebration subsided that the delay to my individual induction the Hall of Fame worked to include my family for this special day and reinforce God's orchestration. I would not have experienced the joy of my daughter hugging my leg after my walk across campus or the movie-like ending after my speech had it happened any year sooner.

Family has always been an important cornerstone in my life: my immediate family, extended family, college family, church family, and those who came into my life to become like family. I could not have appreciated my induction into the Hall of Fame as much as I did had I not seen the impact of all the people God brought into my life—for a season or the long term. Giving up control of my life and enjoying the twists and turns God has planned for my life got me to the destination he wanted me to achieve—the plan God made even before I was born!

He has done that for you too. No matter where you are in life, he has a plan for your life. You choose the roads you travel in life, and the route may or may not be the best way to get to your final destination. Rest assured, God has an infinite amount of patience for you and truly wants the best for you. He will get you to a most spectacular view if you develop the faith and patience to let him take you there, even when you think your way is better.

Trust me when I say your way is not what you need and usually more difficult than the map God has laid out for you. You may not reach an Athletic Hall of Fame in your travels, but your life has a purpose. You may be part of the storyline that creates a cure for cancer, brings lasting peace to the world, or just makes someone's life a little easier and happier. Have faith, enjoy the ride, and keep kicking!

The Farrell "15"

On life's journey, there are road signs to help us with direction and keep us from getting lost. I have taken note of some of these signs, and in honor of my jersey number I've written out fifteen distinct signs I noticed on my road through life. I share these with you in the hope that you can utilize some or all of them to keep your life on track and feel the rich blessings God has available for each and every one of you.

1

Strive for Constant Improvement.

MEDITATION:

Do you not know that in a race all the runners run, but only one gets the prize? Run in such a way as to get the prize.

1 Corinthians 9:24

Internal drive: "Kick through it, not to it." Motivating yourself takes effort. No matter what you do in life, if you strive to improve each day, each hour, whether you are practicing sports, a musical instrument, striving for better grades, or aiming for a better job in your career, you need to make it a point to get better with everything you do.

Don't be complacent or settle. God created you for greatness, but it will take effort and possibly an attitude change to make the most of your life. Highly successful people aim to get better at their tasks in life.

Each day of practice for football, I tried to make my kicking motions and techniques more consistent and methodical. Some days I did not see progress, but I did know the next day I could try something else to get more consistent and improve as a kicker. Drive and desire enable improvement. You can develop internal drive over time, and it will become a cornerstone in making you a better person in whatever path you take in life.

2

Learn from Every Experience

MEDITATION:

Listen to advice and accept discipline, and at
the end you will be counted among the wise.

Proverbs 19:20

We are blessed with opportunities galore during our lives.
The perspective we take will be directly proportional to how successful we will be in life. Whether you are learning how to cook
food, acquiring a new skill at work, or trying to get better at a
sport, you have an opportunity to learn from those around you
and experts in the field.

I watched others to learn how to kick better. I wanted to send
up the ball with the perfect slow rotation—end over end—when
I contacted it. I would also try new techniques during practice to
try to raise my level and become a better kicker for each practice.

Look at the positive from every experience and build upon
your success. You can find something positive in anything you do!

3

Treat Others with Respect

MEDITATION:

Show proper respect to everyone, love the
family of believers, fear God, honor the emperor.

1 Peter 2:17

Be a teammate in all you do. I learned this lesson early in life
and try to live this virtue continuously. Perhaps because of how I
was treated at times, I have always tried to respect others, no matter their station in life—older, younger, richer, poorer, apparently
perfect in every way, or different from me in physical or mental
abilities. The world can always use more respect, starting with
how you treat other people.

When you meet someone new, genuine appreciation for being able to meet and get to know others shows this respect. It also
puts your best foot forward and makes a good impression. My
grandmother once said to me, "You are no better or worse than
anyone else. Everyone puts their pants on one leg at a time. Always keep your head up—except when you are kicking the football." This holds true for everyone.

God created each of us for a purpose. We are all a part of the
Master Plan, and each has a place in this world. Disrespecting
others lessens their potential to make the world a better place.
Total success comes by lifting others with respect, not putting
people down to lift yourself.

You rarely know the immediate purpose of the people who cross your path at the time. Better to build a bridge for a future opportunity than to close that door immediately with surly behavior.

4
Appreciate the Opportunities You Receive

MEDITATION:

And whatever you do, whether in word or deed, do it all in the name of the Lord Jesus, giving thanks to God the Father through him.

Colossians 3:17

You never know when you will be given an opportunity to better yourself. Take advantage of ways you can grow and make a difference, to become someone better who affects the world around you positively.

Look at every opportunity as a chance to become a better person than you were the last time you faced that situation. Occasions for each challenge may be plentiful or limited. You never know how many you will have, so take advantage of each chance to truly improve. to

We are given the option to accept direction or choose our own way. Whatever you decide, appreciate each prospect and how the opportunity could make you a better person or help you improve in the future.

5

Serve Others, Not Self

MEDITATION:

Do nothing out of selfish ambition or vain conceit. Rather, in humility value others above yourselves, not looking to your own interests but each of you to the interests of the others.

Philippians 2:3–4

Avoid being too proud or self-serving; instead, be humble. The bottom line: don't worry about what is in it for you. Instead, consider how you can positively impact someone else's life.

You never know when you will be called on to lift someone to reach their potential. You also never know when you will need someone to lift you to your full potential. Lifting others elevates the whole team or group more quickly to collectively reach higher and to also meet our life's original purpose.

Concentrating on your problems and issues and why you are not achieving your full potential closes you off to new opportunities that can ultimately make you better. Helping others opens the possibilities to make a difference in the world around you. When you build a reputation as a difference-maker, people will look to you to lead. Be the change you want to see in the world.

6

Work Harder Than the Next Guy

MEDITATION:

Whatever you do, work at it with all your
heart,
as working for the Lord, not for human masters,
since you know that you will receive an
inheritance from the Lord as a reward. It is the
Lord Christ you are serving.

Colossians 3:23–24

Whether you are working as a clerk at a grocery store or trying to be the first team kicker on the team, you need to put forth greater effort than your competition. Competition greatly motivates positive behavior. Certain aspects of the next person's performance may be better than yours; however, you can improve and make progress to better yourself. Apply yourself diligently to everything you do. To be your best, control your success by working harder and doing more than the next person in line.

In my case, I practiced kicking an untold number of extra points in practice from all sorts of angles and distances to build consistencyas a kicker. Each day in practice, I had to find something new to improve on to solidify my position as the first-team kicker. I worked harder than the other kickers on the team and in our league. It wasn't easy, and the mental aspects challenged me more than the physical work at times. Each day's challenge led me to realize the potential set before me in God's plan.

149

7

Lift Others to Make the Team Better

MEDITATION:

Therefore encourage one another and build
each other up, just as in fact you are doing.

I Thessalonians 5:11

No matter what you do or where you work, you work with
other people. When my teammates were on the field, I encouraged them from the sidelines. After I attempted a kick, I'd always
take the time to thank the holder and long snapper for their efforts and our blockers for doing their job.

When you are part of a team, the success you enjoy is not
based on one person; it is a collective effort to achieve your destiny. Being part of a team isn't exclusive to sports. Any collection
of people bound together for a common purpose forms a team—
from study groups to workplace teams to common-cause teams
to the "human team" we all are part of here on earth.

When you encourage other team members and everyone participates with the same passion and purpose to lift others, success
can almost be guaranteed. Positivity creates an atmosphere for
excellence. Such a powerful force cannot be stopped and will continue to feed success and bring forth a winning attitude for all to
enjoy.

8

Keep a Positive Attitude

MEDITATION:

I can do all this through him who gives me strength.

Philippians 4:13

Especially when things look the darkest, keep a positive attitude. Life will provide twists and turns and detours on the journey of life. You will always find what you are looking for— good or bad.

Looking at the positive side of life enables a joyful journey and builds on success. Life is an amazing thing, and the choices you make will provide multiple opportunities.

Sometimes you will make choices that don't have the best long-term effect. Desiring what others preach to be the best may not be ideal for your life journey. For me, I fixated on playing Division I football, assuming it would be best for me, but that wasn't part of God's plan. When I kept fixating on that, seeing that trajectory wasn't working out in my favor made me anxious. I couldn't see the total picture nor the other options available to me.

If I was truly objective, I could see the best path for me to take included a school with a quality program in my chosen degree and a close-knit community of people who would better fit my personality and long-term growth. Seeking the positives allowed me to see better opportunities for my life. A positive outlook kept me on a

151

more upward trajectory for my emotional, scholastic, and athletic endeavors.

9

Follow God's Plan for Your Life

MEDITATION:

Many are the plans in a person's heart,
    but it is the LORD's purpose that prevails.

Proverbs 19:21

Communicate with God, and do a lot of listening. This point can be one of the most difficult to follow, but once you understand the dynamic, it can be one of the most gratifying experiences of all. The difficulty comes in "knowing" the plan for your life exactly. If you think about it, the best way to find out about plans for work or school or to get directions on a trip when you are lost is to ask.

Sometimes you need to ask what your role in the plan consists of several times until you understand it. In your life, you need to be open to the plan and your role, and this is no different. The major difference is, you are speaking to God this time, and he usually doesn't guide you with an audible voice.

Don't get me wrong, he *will* communicate with you and guide you when you genuinely communicate with him. It may be a sign in nature, a feeling in your soul, or a person who crosses your path at the most opportune time. You will have to be open to these signs, look for them, and continue talking with God in prayer (or any form that allows you to connect with him) to find your plan. Finding God's plan is not easy, but it is possible when you keep the lines of communication open and keep seeking honestly.

Not only is patience a virtue, but in this case, it is a necessity. God reveals things in his time, not ours. It took me several years of seeking to begin to see the plan, and even then, I only put together bits and pieces for a while.

Your timing may be longer or shorter, depending on your communication level and listening patience. If you honestly seek your purpose, you will find God's purpose for your life.

10
Celebrate the Positive

Don't get too high or too low emotionally. There are experiences throughout life that are positive and others that are negative. When you experience something positive, celebrate it in some way. Tell a friend or family member, take a minute to relish your success, tell yourself how proud you are of your results. The celebration doesn't have to be a stop-the-world and receive-the-adulation-of-others type of recognition. Learn to reinforce positive experiences so it becomes your habit to look for the positives.

You will find what you seek . . . you might as well seek the positives in life. Life is so much better when you enjoy what is happening to you! Something as simple as a sunrise or brilliantly colored sunset can reach deep into your soul and bring you inner peace and satisfaction.

I began to seek positive things during my senior year in high school, and I found so many wonders I had never noticed. It is amazing how your outlook will change when you see the success your actions produce.

11

Be Part of a Team

MEDITATION:

Above all, love each other deeply, because love
covers over a multitude of sins. Offer hospitality
to one another without grumbling. Each of you
should use whatever gift you have received to
serve others, as faithful stewards of God's grace in
its various forms.

1 Peter 4:8–10

Don't try to do everything by yourself. People generally think
that, to be successful, you must do all the work yourself, or it is
not a true success. My take is, we are not on this planet alone,
therefore we were put together to work as a team to achieve real
success.

Being a part of a team is a good thing as long as there is trust
and all memberssupport the common goal. As a kicker, I was
part of a unit that had ten other people working to make extra
point attempts succeed. I would not have achieved my success
unless there was a long snapper who snapped the ball back to the
holder, and a holder who placed the ball so I could kick it, and
other teammates who blocked the opponents. All the members
coordinated so I could have a chance to do my job—kick the ball
through the uprights. If one person didn't do his job, the unit did
not succeed.

This applies to life as well. Life is easier when you have a team working for the success of everyone. Though sometimes you have to face off against the world alone, so many other times when you can team up and conquer a task with others and achieve your objectives.

12

Understand You Have a Place in Life

MEDITATION:

"For I know the plans I have for you," declares the LORD, "plans to prosper you and not to harm you, plans to give you hope and a future."

Jeremiah 29:11

You were created uniquely and for a purpose. Each and every one of us was created for a purpose by God. Life challenges us to understand what that purpose is. Finding your purpose comes easier to some than others, but it is not impossible.

Life is a precious thing and not to be taken for granted. You may not set a record, but you may be the person who inspires a record holder. You may develop the next great vaccine, or you might inspire the person who creates the next great vaccine. Your purpose could be to develop a safe and nurturing environment that will help produce the next great athlete, scientist, doctor, pastor, or artist! You might never know for certain when your purpose is being exercised, and that is alright. When you strive to do the right thing at all times and keep a humble, servant attitude toward others, you will achieve the greatness God has planned for you! You were created for a reason, and God has a plan for your success!

13

Dream **Big**

MEDITATION:

Commit to the LORD whatever you do, and
he will establish your plans.

Proverbs 16:3

You cannot out-dream what God has planned for your life.
When you truly have a heart for doing the right thing, God will
show you a life you could never see standing in one place. When
you try to live by the ideals of giving to others and having a humble nature, life will open to you in ways you can never imagine.

God has plans for your life, and these plans are so much
richer than what we may want for ourselves. God knows our capabilities and our needs, which differ from our wants. Give an
honest look at your capabilities and where you fit into the scheme
of things, and then seek the highest level of success you can. Seek
the pieces of the puzzle that will enhance your value to the dream.

In anything there will be a sacrifice, perhaps something personal or something out of your comfort zone. When you sacrifice
to follow God's plan for your life, it will bring you closer to dream
fulfillment.

14

Do Not Hinge Success on **Your** Wants

MEDITATION:

To humans belong the plans of the heart, but from the LORD comes the proper answer of the tongue.

Proverbs 16:1

Success is directly proportional to how you live your life. Success comes in many forms. Some consider great wealth or popularity true success. Others promote self-actualization and inner peace as true measures of success. I believe true success comes from how you lead your life, not what you want for yourself.

Lead a life of service to others and promote actions that provide success for the "team." If you think you are not part of a team may I suggest we are all part of the human team here on earth! Success is not a reward for selfishness.

True success comes from making the world a better place for others, even when it feels like an insignificant act on your part. You may not know at the time what impact you can have on others' lives or plans. God has a plan for your success, and it may not be what you want. Happiness and true success will come when you align with God's plan for your life.

15

Express Appreciation to Others as Life Goes On

MEDITATION:

As iron sharpens iron, so one person sharpens another.

Proverbs 27:17

Do not wait to tell others how much you appreciate their effect on your life. As you make your way through life, you will be in contact with people who make a difference to you or set you in a positive direction in line with God's plan for your life. You need to recognize these special people and tell them how they positively affected your life.

Depending on the timing, you may find this simple act can lift their life and yours as well. Many people will not recognize the time when they made a difference in your life unless you tell them. This news may come at a time when they need it most. Maybe it will confirm their purpose in life.

When you can share examples of how others have assisted your successes, it will bring a positive feeling to both of you to share that experience. A simple "thank you" and a smile can go a long way in showing appreciation and lifting others up. Expressing your appreciation also makes you feel good and spreads more positivity in the world.

Was it destiny that I kick barefoot?

Detroit Lions and NFL great, Eddie Murray stops by practice in Fenton as I sneak up on the ball. Of course I had a clean uniform.

MIKE FARRELL

Standard press release photo from Adrian College.

1983 All American Certificate

1985 All American Certificate

167

'One Good Thing' Challenge

When I was struggling most with my internal demons, I was wallowing in a personal negative spiral of darkness and finding every negative aspect of life. One of the best ways I was able to turn my life around was to find 'One Good Thing' each day to turn my outlook on life to the positive. It was a difficult challenge at first as I was trying to do it alone and hiding my shame and depression. The best medicine I experienced was finding 'One Good Thing' each day to find the positive side of life. My journey would have been easier if I would have opened up and had others helping me seek the positive. Positive changes accelerated when I found more people who shared a positive outlook. I challenge you to be a part of a new community of support. Share 'One Good Thing' that happened to you today. Your daily share can be something as simple as a sunset you saw that touched you in a positive way; a blessing you received from a friend or a total stranger; the peaceful breeze on a warm summer night; or something that has special meaning to you. You can find 'One Good Thing' each day. The more you look for it, the more 'Good Things' you will begin to find each day and as a result, will look for opportunities for you to be the Good in the world! Join the challenge and share your experiences on our website www.barefootkicker.com and we will provide a list for others to see and aspire to find their 'Good Thing' each day!

About the Author

Michael Farrell, a life thriver, was raised in the suburbs of DC had a rather standard upbringing while dealing with growing social anxiety. His life thrived in his secure social bubble until life changed at 13 years of age with a move to Michigan and a new life. His involvement in sports, scouts, and faith were the path to positive enlightenment and overcoming his anxieties. As a graduate of Adrian College participating in the storied football program and the first Adrian team to participate in the NCAA Division III national playoffs. Mike went on to build a successful career in Materials Management, married and built a family through adoption and became an award-winning advocate for adoptive families.